The Military History of
REVOLUTIONARY
WAR LAND
BATTLES

The Military History of

Revolutionary War Land Battles

by T. N. DUPUY, Col., U.S. Army (Ret.)
and GAY M. HAMMERMAN

Illustrated with maps by Dyno Lowenstein

FRANKLIN WATTS | NEW YORK | LONDON

SBN 531 01258-1

Copyright © 1970 by Franklin Watts, Inc.
Library of Congress Catalog Card Number: 79–110470
Printed in the United States of America
2   3   4   5

FOR JONNA AND HERB

Contents

The Military History of
REVOLUTIONARY
WAR LAND
BATTLES

Introduction—A War Begins at Boston

"Taxation Without Representation"

Boston in April of 1775 was a city dead to trade and commerce, cut off from the outside world through the closing of its port. Otherwise, however, it was very much alive; alive with rumor, watchful eyes, and concealed activity.

This situation was the result of twelve years of blunders and misunderstandings. The government of King George III of Great Britain was determined that the people of the thirteen colonies of British North America should pay for the administration, security, and protection provided them by the mother country. It seemed only right to the British Parliament that the proper way for the colonists to make this payment was through the fair and democratic method of taxation.

The colonists, on the other hand, were people who had left England, or whose fathers had left England, because they sought greater freedom in the New World. They were as jealous of that freedom as they were proud of their British heritage. As free Britons, they were determined that they would not pay for, or accept, any obligations imposed upon them by a legislature

3

three thousand miles away. "Taxation without representation is tyranny," they said.

Colonial indignation had mounted in the years since 1763, as the British Parliament's Sugar Act had followed the Molasses Act, and the Townshend Acts of 1767 had followed the Stamp Act of 1765. To avoid payment of taxes on many goods covered by the Townshend Acts, a great number of colonists refused to buy products made in England, and began to smuggle goods in from other countries. Local colonial governments sent appeals and petitions to the king and to Parliament; local groups of citizens, as well as congresses and assemblies representing several colonies, met to assert their rights as British subjects. The British government was equally determined that the laws should be enforced; Parliament was convinced that the colonists were trying to avoid financial responsibility by placing the burdens of colonial administration and security upon the people of England.

The people of Massachusetts took the lead in colonial opposition to the increasingly harsh enforcement measures imposed by the British government. British troops were sent to Boston in 1768, leading to disorders that culminated in the so-called Boston Massacre in 1770. Violence and repression stimulated still stronger opposition among the colonists, particularly in Massachusetts. In 1772, under the leadership of Samuel Adams, local "Committees of Correspondence" were secretly formed, to begin planning for the use of force if necessary to protect their rights as Englishmen. Similar committees were soon formed in other colonies.

There was an outcry in all of the colonies when it was learned that the colonies would have to pay a special heavy duty on tea,

The BLOODY MASSACRE perpetrated in King—¦—Street BOSTON on March 5.¹ 1770 by a party of the 29th REG.ᵗ

Unhappy Boston! see thy Sons deplore,
Thy hallow'd Walks besmear'd with guiltless Gore.
While faithless P—n. and his savage Bands,
With murd'rous Rancour stretch their bloody Hands;
Like fierce Barbarians grinning o'er their Prey.
Approve the Carnage and enjoy the Day.

If scalding drops from Rage from Anguish Wrung
If speechless Sorrows lab'ring for a Tongue,
Or if a weeping World can ought appease
The plaintive Ghosts of Victims such as these;
The Patriot's copious Tears for each are shed,
A glorious Tribute which embalms the Dead.

But know Fate summons to that awful Goal,
Where Justice strips the Murd'rer of his Soul:
Should venal C—ts the scandal of the Land,
Snatch the relentless Villain from her Hand,
Keen Execrations on this Plate inscrib'd,
Shall reach a Judge who never can be brib'd

Engrav'd Printed & Sold by Paul Revere Boston

The unhappy Sufferers were Mess.ʳˢ Sam.ˡ Gray, Sam.ˡ Maverick, Jam.ˢ Caldwell, Crispus Attucks & Pat.ᵏ Carr
Killed. Six wounded; two of them (Christ.ʳ Monk & John Clark) Mortally

Boston Massacre, March 5, 1770. Of this event John Adams later wrote: "On that day the formation of American Independence was laid. . . . Not the Battle of Lexington or Bunker Hill, nor the surrender of Burgoyne or Cornwallis were more important events in American History than the Battle of King Street. . . ." Note that in Paul Revere's engraving the dead man closest to the British was a Negro; this was Crispus Attucks, one of the leaders of the Patriot demonstrators, who was cut down by two British musket balls. (New York Public Library)

although no such tax was being levied in England. The outcry became outrage when, soon afterward, large cargoes of tea arrived in colonial ports. Massachusetts again took the lead in active response; on December 16, 1773, citizens of Boston, dressed as Indians, boarded the tea ships and dumped the cargoes in the harbor in the "Boston Tea Party."

The Coercive Acts

It was the turn of the British government to be outraged. It responded with the "Coercive Acts," closing the port of Boston, sending more troops to be garrisoned in the city to terrorize its inhabitants, and repealing many of the people's traditional and treasured rights as British subjects.

Although the people of Boston were helpless under the iron control of the British Crown, things were humming elsewhere in Massachusetts, and in other colonies as well. In August and September, 1774, a convention of Massachusetts citizens met at Suffolk. The convention adopted a series of "Resolves" prepared by Dr. Joseph Warren, denouncing the Coercive Acts and calling for economic action and military preparation to resist them. Massachusetts leaders urged the other colonies to support the Suffolk Resolves, and to defend their liberty by force, if necessary. Committees of Safety were soon established, prepared to take over the functions of government in the event of rebellion.

Colonists who plunged ever more actively into preparations to preserve their liberty by force if necessary called themselves "Patriots"; they were opposed by the "Loyalists" who were horri-

6

fied by the thought of violence or rebellion against the Crown. There was a more or less even division between Patriots and Loyalists throughout the thirteen colonies, save in Massachusetts, where the Patriots predominated and controlled most of the local governments.

Representatives of all of the colonies met at Philadelphia in September and October of 1774 in the First Continental Congress. They prepared a petition asking King George to recognize colonial rights. The radical Patriots of Massachusetts, meanwhile, were organizing themselves for more direct action. They took control of the colony's 30 militia regiments; one-fourth of the men of each regiment were appointed "minutemen," to be prepared to take up their arms to fight at a minute's notice. In open defiance of British authority, these militiamen trained and drilled on their village greens.

Commanding the British garrison in Boston was General Thomas Gage, the overall commander of all British forces in the American colonies. Grimly he kept track of the activities going on throughout Massachusetts. He had reliable informants among the leaders of the colonial resistance movement—secret Loyalists who pretended to be Patriots. He knew how much ammunition the colonists had collected; and he could draw maps of the places in the town of Concord where most of their arms and supplies were hidden. Similarly, the rebellious colonists had many willing agents of their own among the citizens of Boston, who constantly reported the movements of General Gage's highly visible red-coated soldiers.

CHAPTER 1

Lexington and Concord

Gage's Plan

During the early months of 1775, food, money, and formal resolutions of support poured in to Boston from the other colonies through narrow Boston Neck. In view of this evidence of colonial solidarity, and with the provincial militia gaining daily in training and arms, the British government decided that the time had come to strike hard and decisively to end all rebellious activity. On April 14, General Thomas Gage received instructions from London to take immediate steps to disrupt any treasonable colonial plans.

General Gage did not believe that he had enough troops to suppress a full-scale revolt in Massachusetts, and it would be several weeks before he could receive the reinforcements he had requested. He did know, however, where the rebel arms were stored, and he decided to seize them quickly. He feared that if he waited until the reinforcements arrived the rebels would learn his plans and move their munitions.

Gage ordered Lieutenant Colonel Francis Smith to take 700 men to Concord to destroy the rebel guns, ammunitions, and supplies. These were picked troops—the elite grenadier and light infantry companies of each of the regiments of the Boston garrison. They were to embark at the Back Bay at 10:00 P.M. on April 18, go by boat across the Charles River, and then through Cambridge and on to Concord. They were then to return "as soon as possible." Smith was given a map showing the hiding places of the supplies and arms. Gage ordered him not to permit any plundering or damaging of private property.

The Rebel Alert

Gage had chosen the water route out of Boston because it offered more hope of secrecy than a march down the Boston Neck. But even so, surprise would be difficult. Many people saw boats being gathered from all the British ships in Boston Harbor to transport the men across the bay. Paul Revere, a silversmith and active Patriot, had a private intelligence corps of thirty

Boston and Vicinity.

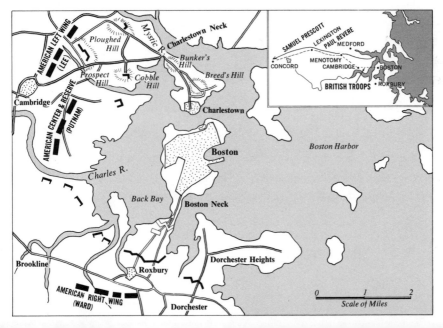

people who continually kept watch for suspicious British movements in Boston. Revere's superior in the rebel intelligence network was Dr. Joseph Warren, author of the Suffolk Resolves and Boston's liaison man with the Concord Committee of Safety. When Warren got word of the impending move he immediately alerted Revere. He also sent William Dawes, another active Patriot, off to Lexington to warn rebel leaders John Hancock and Samuel Adams, and then on to alert the Patriots at Concord, four miles farther. Dawes took the Boston Neck road, the long way around. Revere was to take the shorter route, crossing the Charles River ahead of the British.

After dark on the evening of April 18, Revere was rowed to Charlestown, directly north of Boston, and was met there by a fellow conspirator with a good horse. Revere took off for Lexington and Concord, rousing the militia leaders of the towns he passed through. A British patrol stopped both him and Dawes on the far side of Lexington, but Dr. Samuel Prescott, another Patriot who had joined them, got through to alert the Patriots at Concord.

As Colonel Smith and his men marched through the dark towns and countryside, they could tell by the ringing church bells, signaling musket shots, and running footsteps that their passage was no secret. Smith sent a message back to Gage asking for reinforcements. The general had in fact already ordered the 1st Brigade and a battalion of marines—1,000 men in all—to leave at 4:00 A.M. to support Smith. It was 9:00 A.M., however, before they actually got away.

Fighting at Lexington

The British advance guard, under Royal Marine Major John Pitcairn, reached Lexington at dawn. There they were met by seventy minutemen of the town, drawn up in two lines across the Common. Pitcairn was anxious to avoid bloodshed. He ordered the Americans to disperse and told his own men to hold their fire. Some of the minutemen began to drift away, but suddenly a shot rang out, probably from a rebel musket.

Pitcairn tried to restrain the British, but one of his platoons fired a volley, and the others followed. As some of the Americans were beginning to answer with individual aimed shots, the British followed their musket volley with a bayonet charge. The Americans fled, taking ten wounded men with them and leaving eight dead on the Common. The British had only one man wounded. Their spirits high, the troops marched on toward Concord to the sound of fife and drum.

At the Bridge

Colonel Smith's objective, the hidden arms and supplies, had almost disappeared by the time he reached Concord. Warned by earlier rumors, and alerted by Dr. Prescott three hours before the British arrived, the Patriots of Concord had quickly moved them to new hiding places.

As the British approached, the militia leader, James Barrett, gathered his men on Punkatasset Hill, north of the village and west of the Concord River. Colonel Smith sent six companies of light infantry to guard the North Bridge across the river, and

11

another company to guard the South Bridge. Then the rest of the British began their search. They found only a few gun carriages, some other equipment, and a few barrels of flour. They rolled the barrels into the millpond, and burned much of the other equipment.

The burning set fire to the courthouse and blacksmith shop. Although the British moved quickly to put out the fires, the Americans watching from the hill could see only the smoke. Thinking they were witnessing a scene of wanton plunder and destruction, they began to load their muskets and move down toward the North Bridge. There were by then only three British companies at the bridge, for the others had moved across the river to the Barrett Farm in search of rebel weapons.

The militia moved forward, led by the company of Captain Isaac Davis from the village of Acton. Outnumbered, the British bridge guard moved back across the river and opened fire. The Americans, spreading out in a skirmish line, returned the fire with accurate sharpshooting, and the British withdrew hastily into the village. Expecting a counterattack, the Americans waited at a stone wall, out of musket range from the bridge. The three British companies returning from Barrett Farm got by them and crossed the bridge with no difficulty.

Colonel Smith seems to have been uncertain as to what to do next. He had lost three men killed and nine wounded in the skirmish, while the Americans had lost two dead and two wounded. The aimed American fire had been more effective than at Lexington. It was significant that four of the wounded British were officers, whose gleaming epaulets and gold lace made them good targets. Smith finally decided that his men

12

had found and destroyed all the stores they were likely to. At noon he ordered them to move out for Boston.

The Road Back

It was a hot day. The British troops had been up all night, and they were nearing exhaustion after their twenty miles' march, two skirmishes, and the frustrating search of Concord. But the worst of the day was still ahead of them.

The Concord minutemen followed the British column as it moved toward Lexington. They were behind it and on both sides, but always just out of musket range. Smith placed protective flanking detachments on both sides of the road; the main column was preceded by an advance guard and followed by a rear guard. A mile out of Concord, at Merriam's Corner, a new group of minutemen approached from a road to the left. The British detachment covering the left flank, nerves tensed by the skulking militia on all sides of them, opened fire. The little American force fired back, and then the surrounding militiamen joined the fight.

The British were not yet trained to deal with this kind of attack. They were armed with the "brown Bess" musket, which did not even have a rear sight to make accurate aiming possible. They had been taught to fire as a unit, pointing their weapons, rather than aiming them, at a massed group of enemy soldiers. The unorthodox American tactics gave them no targets to shoot at.

Smith had planned to group his men for a stand when they

13

RETREAT OF THE BRITISH   FROM LEXINGTON

Retreat of the British from Lexington, April 19, 1775. This stylized engraving, probably dating from about a century after the event, is inaccurate in its details but captures the spirit of the day. (Charles Phelps Cushing)

reached Lexington. But by the time they got there the depleted rear guard was about to be overwhelmed; ammunition was running low, Smith himself was wounded, and Pitcairn was thrown from his horse when the animal was grazed by a musket ball. In some confusion the British continued their retreat through Lexington. They had struggled a mile down the road

14

toward the next town, Menotomy, when they suddenly found temporary safety.

The reinforcements General Gage had ordered, 1,000 men under Brigadier General Earl Hugh Percy, had finally reached Menotomy. Smith's exhausted men filtered through Percy's line and fell to the ground for rest. The pursuing Americans again halted just beyond range of the British muskets. After giving Smith's men a few minutes to catch their breaths, Percy ordered a retreat to Boston.

The British ordeal was not yet finished, however. By the time Percy reached Cambridge he realized that his entire command was in real danger. Thousands of Americans were hovering all around his column. If he took the Charles River bridge at Cambridge and went on to the Boston Neck, he might be disastrously delayed. The bridge had been partly destroyed by Patriot agents the night before, and repairing it had delayed Percy on his way to Lexington. He could not risk the possibility that the rebels had done more damage, and that his outnumbered force might be blocked at the Charles while American marksmen picked off his waiting men.

Percy therefore turned sharply northeast, marched his men over the Charlestown Neck, and placed them on the high ground of Bunker's Hill, commanding the narrow neck. Here the British had a formidable position. The Americans did not try to pursue across the neck. It was now nightfall, and the first day of fighting in the American Revolution had ended.

It was a day in which about 4,000 ill-organized and poorly disciplined American militiamen had repulsed 1,700 British regulars. The British had learned some of the strengths and weaknesses of the Americans they would be fighting, especially

15

the power of the aimed American musket. They had lost 65 dead, 173 wounded, and 26 missing, while the Americans had lost 49 dead and 46 wounded or missing.

All through the night that followed, men of Massachusetts took up their guns and gathered with their militia companies. Others rode out to spread the word through the colonies.

CHAPTER 2

Bunker Hill

A Hill Is Fortified

Militia units from the rest of Massachusetts and from other New England colonies began to gather after the fighting at Lexington and Concord. Their immediate military objective was to bottle up the British garrison in the city of Boston. The Americans, commanded by General Artemas Ward, the senior Massachusetts militia officer, blocked the Boston Neck, the only overland approach to the city. Since the Royal Navy controlled the water that almost surrounded Boston, the British could not be isolated from supplies, or be prevented from leaving the city by sea. But as long as Boston Neck was blocked, they could be kept from launching a land attack into the surrounding countryside.

Nearby, and accessible by water from the Boston peninsula, were two commanding heights that the British might seize and fortify, thus threatening American control of the land approaches to the city. One of these was a series of three hills on the Charlestown peninsula due north of Boston; the other was Dorchester Heights to the southeast. Early in June the rebels learned from their spies that General Gage was planning to seize these areas. The Massachusetts Provincial Congress at

17

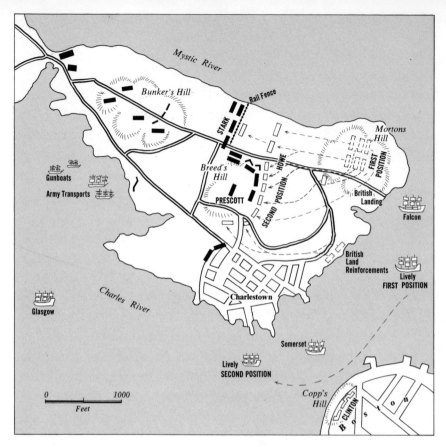

Battle of Bunker Hill.

once ordered General Ward to move in ahead of the British. First, he was to occupy and fortify Bunker's Hill, the highest point on the Charlestown peninsula. Dorchester Heights would be dealt with later.

Ward was reluctant to obey this order. He felt that the colonial army was too undisciplined and lacking in unity to attempt such an aggressive move at that time. He had no power of command over any but Massachusetts troops, although units

18

from Connecticut, Rhode Island, and New Hampshire had joined the besieging force. He called a council of war of the senior rebel officers, hoping to win support for his view that the project should be canceled. Ward was outvoted, however. Colonel William Prescott of Pepperell, Massachusetts, was ordered to take a force to fortify Bunker's Hill during the night of June 16.

Prescott and his command of about 1,200 men set out from Cambridge just after nightfall and marched across the narrow Charlestown Neck. They were accompanied by Brigadier General Israel Putnam of Connecticut, who had no command role on the expedition but had come along because he had been one of the strongest advocates of the fortification project. When they reached the heights of the Charlestown Peninsula, an argument developed between Putnam and Prescott. Putnam insisted that the critical military feature of the peninsula was not Bunker's Hill, but rather Breed's Hill, which was slightly lower, but was 600 yards nearer Boston. Prescott reluctantly accepted Putnam's position, and the men began digging on Breed's Hill. By morning they had produced a redoubt 130 feet square and 6 feet high.

British Reaction

At dawn a British sloop in the harbor spotted the new landmark and opened fire. In Boston the senior British officers met in hurried council to decide on action. In addition to Gage, there were Major Generals William Howe, Henry Clinton, and John ("Gentleman Johnny") Burgoyne. By fortifying Breed's

19

Hill instead of Bunker's Hill, the Americans had, knowingly or not, issued a challenge that the British generals could not ignore. Bunker's Hill was out of artillery range of the harbor, but guns on Breed's Hill could strike the British ships.

Clinton urged that a small force be landed behind the rebels on Charlestown Neck, to starve them out without bloodshed. Howe disagreed. He felt that the challenge should be met promptly and forcefully. He recommended an immediate assault, and Gage decided in his favor. Howe was to lead the assault force himself. The plan was to land at the southeast end of the peninsula, march along its Mystic River side out of musket range of the redoubt, and then attack it from the rear. The British began embarking at noon.

Shortly after daybreak Prescott began to realize how dangerous his situation was. He pushed his men hard to build an additional earthwork that would run about 300 feet northeastward from the redoubt to protect the left flank. Many of his men could also see that the exposed American position was in danger. Some of the frightened militiamen deserted, and Putnam rode back to Cambridge to get reinforcements from General Ward. Reluctantly, Ward sent two New Hampshire regiments, commanded by Colonels John Stark and James Reed. Before they could leave, however, they had to melt lead for musket balls, and make up cartridges. Under Stark's overall command, they set out for Charlestown at noon, the same time that the British were embarking in Boston.

It was a little after 1:00 P.M. when the first British boats landed just east of Moulton's (or Morton's) Hill, near the tip of the peninsula. As General Howe's boat touched shore he saw the reinforcing columns of the New Hampshire regiments

20

arriving on the north side of the peninsula, and realized that his planned enveloping movement might have to be modified. To secure the landing area, he immediately sent a battalion toward Charlestown under Brigadier General Sir George Pigot, and four companies straight forward over Moulton's Hill.

The American Defenses

There was an American company in Charlestown to protect Prescott's right flank. As Pigot's men approached, the Americans opened fire. Shot from the ships in the harbor and from a battery in Boston itself had been sporadically falling on the American positions all day. Now the fire of all of these guns converged in Charlestown. Some of the projectiles were hot shot (cannon-balls heated red hot before being fired); the village went up in flames.

By noon Prescott had only 500 men left out of the 1,200 he had started with. The others, never under fire before and without real discipline or training, had gradually melted away during the morning. What Prescott had left was his own regiment of 300 men from Groton, Acton, and Pepperell, and 200 of General Putnam's Connecticut troops under Captain Thomas Knowlton. Many of these were veterans of the French and Indian War, and could be counted on to stay under fire. During the early afternoon the American force began to grow again, as the New Hampshire reinforcements came up, along with a few committed Patriots who heard a battle was taking shape and wanted to participate.

Prescott, realizing that his left flank was exposed, and that the British could get behind him by moving through the area between the new breastwork and the Mystic River shore, had sent Knowlton's Connecticut men to take up positions behind a stone and rail fence that ran eastward beyond the breastwork. They had thrown up another rough rail fence behind it and stuffed handfuls of mown hay in between the two to make an insubstantial breastwork. The gap between this and Prescott's earth breastwork was filled by several small V-shaped trenches. However, there was still space on the beach for enemy troops to pass.

As Stark advanced with his New Hampshire regiment, he saw the gap between Knowlton's men and the Mystic River shore. He could also see that the British seemed to be grouping for an attack in this direction. Stark moved his regiments into the open area, barricaded the beach with large rocks, and placed his best men to guard it. The rest of the New Hampshire men were deployed to the right rear to reinforce Knowlton.

There were now once more about 1,200 Americans on the peninsula. They were divided into three separate groups—the Charlestown village detachment, now scattered behind the burning village, but still ready to fight; Prescott's men in the redoubt and behind the earthen breastwork; and the men of Knowlton's and Stark's commands at the fence and on the beach. There was no communication between these groups; Prescott's orders could carry no farther than his voice.

Howe had revised his plan in view of the suddenly strengthened rebel left flank. His main attack would be an assault on the rail fence area with a secondary bayonet attack on the American left by a detachment of light infantry moving along the shoreline. A third force, under General Pigot, was to move in on the main redoubt from the British left.

The Americans watched the red-coated British coming. Under the urging of their officers the undisciplined militiamen held their fire until the attackers were well within musket range. "Don't fire until you see the whites of their eyes!" is the order attributed to Putnam at this time.

The British lines climbing the hill stopped twice to fire volleys, as the Americans still held their fire. The first American fire was from the beach, where Howe's flank attack was stopped by Stark's men. After three attacks were shattered by accurate musket fire, the British on the beach turned and ran.

Meanwhile the men at the rail fence had opened fire when the British to their front were less than 30 yards away. At this range their aimed fire was deadly. In a few moments every officer on Howe's personal staff fell killed or wounded. At the redoubt, also, the first attack was hurled back.

Howe and Pigot rallied their men for a second try. This time they concentrated on the redoubt and breastwork. Again point-blank aimed fire of American muskets shattered the British lines and forced them back out of range.

British losses in the assaulting units were now almost 40 percent. It is a tribute to British training and discipline that Howe could again rally the survivors. The British artillery, which had

23

Battle of Bunker Hill, June 17, 1775. Connecticut troops man the rail fence in the left-center of the American position. The officer on horseback is probably General Israel Putnam; the one on foot is probably Major Thomas Knowlton. It was at this time that Putnam may have shouted his famous order: "Don't fire until you see the whites of their eyes!" To the right rear are the defenses on the hill itself; in the distance, across the mouth of the Charles River, lies Boston. (Charles Phelps Cushing)

been silent through most of the battle because a blunder had supplied it with the wrong ammunition, now opened fire with deadly effectiveness as Howe ordered another assault. He and Pigot led simultaneous bayonet attacks on the redoubt.

Again the Americans placed withering musket fire on the British. Again many fell, among them Major Pitcairn, who had commanded at Lexington. But the stubborn British kept on coming, with fixed bayonets. At this moment the Americans ran out of powder; they clubbed their otherwise useless muskets or threw stones.

Pigot's men crossed the redoubt ditch and scrambled over the parapet. With his men falling about him to British bayonets, Prescott ordered a retreat, and the survivors quickly rushed out of the redoubt, over and past Bunker's Hill, and across the Charlestown Neck to safety. One of those killed in the redoubt was Dr. Joseph Warren. A man the colonies could ill afford to lose, he was one of the volunteers who had come to Breed's Hill because he felt his place was in the battle.

A Myth Is Born

American casualty figures, very rough estimates, were 140 killed, 370 wounded, and 30 taken prisoner, out of a total of perhaps 1,500 who participated in the battle at one time or another. The British, of a strength of about 2,400, lost 226 killed and 838 wounded. These terribly heavy British losses were the result of British blunders as well as American valor and marksmanship. Especially disastrous was Howe's decision to make a frontal attack on the redoubt, rather than following Clinton's plan of starving out the entrenched rebels.

A tactical success for the British, the wrongly named* Battle of Bunker Hill was a great psychological victory for the Americans. It was the first real battle of the war, and in it American farmers had for several hours of hot fighting held off a superior force of first-class British regulars. However, this accomplishment had almost disastrous consequences later. A myth emerged from the true tales of valor of Bunker Hill—the myth that American courage, patriotism, native intelligence, and well-aimed shot could make up for lack of discipline, organization, and military training.

* Twice wrongly named: the battle actually took place on Breed's Hill, and Bunker's Hill was the correct name of the hill where the American redoubt should have been constructed.

CHAPTER 3

Long Island

Rebellion Becomes War

At Philadelphia, on the day before the Battle of Bunker Hill, General George Washington had been appointed commander of all American forces by the Second Continental Congress. He promptly joined the disorganized collection of militia units blockading Boston, and during the rest of 1775, and early 1776, slowly brought shape and order into the newly created Continental Army. In March, Washington seized Dorchester Heights, where heavy artillery, brought overland from captured Fort Ticonderoga, threatened Boston Harbor and the sea approaches to Boston. General Howe, who had succeeded Gage in command at Boston, decided to pull out of the city.

Meanwhile, after initial success, an American invasion of Canada was repulsed at Quebec on December 31, 1776. Young Colonel Benedict Arnold, who had proven himself a brilliant and dynamic leader, was wounded in the assault, but continued to distinguish himself as the ragged invasion army was forced back to Lake Champlain by reinforcements arriving from Britain.

After the British evacuated Boston on March 17, 1776, Washington went to New York, which he expected would become the target for the first British offensive of the war. The British high command had, in fact, already made the decision to seize New York, which was centrally located, had a magnificent harbor, and would provide a base for a thrust up the Hudson that would split the rebellious colonies in half. Admiral Lord Richard Howe was put at the head of the great land and naval expeditionary force being formed in England for the invasion: a fleet of 10 ships of the line, 20 frigates, and several hundred transports, manned by 10,000 British sailors and carrying 32,000 professional soldiers, the largest expeditionary force that had ever been sent out from Great Britain. Lord Richard's brother, General Sir William Howe, would join the expedition at Halifax, to become leader of the army contingent.

The Defense of New York

On June 25 the first ships of the British armada appeared off Sandy Hook, at the entrance to New York Bay. Soon afterward General Howe's troops began to land on Staten Island. To meet the juggernaut, Washington had all too few resources. After repeated pleas to the Continental Congress, by mid-August he had only 20,000 troops, half of whom were relatively reliable Continental soldiers, the rest being short-term militiamen. Washington organized his men into five divisions, commanded by Major General Putnam (who had been at Bunker's Hill), Brigadier General Joseph Spencer, Major General John Sullivan, Brigadier General William Heath, and Major General Nathanael Greene.

Washington's defense plan was designed to deter and delay

28

the British, but not to try to hold New York at all costs. A last-ditch defense against combined land and sea power was not realistic, he decided. The city would be almost impossible to hold because the enemy could make use of a complex network of channels, gulfs, bays, and islands. Attempting to defend the city as best he could, Washington had hulks sunk in Buttermilk Channel and the lower East River; together with Governors Island, these formed an effective barrier at the entrance of the East River. Earthworks, batteries, and barricades were built all around lower Manhattan Island, at key points across the Hudson and East rivers, and at several other places farther up Manhattan. To protect the approach to the city from Long Island, fortifications were built on Brooklyn Heights.

In July the defenders of New York learned that they had a new cause—independence from England. Washington read the news of the Declaration of Independence to his men on July 9.

Lord Howe made his first move on July 12, when he sent two frigates up the Hudson, largely to test the city's defenses. He must have been reassured, for most of the ill-trained American artillerymen never manned their guns, and the few shots that were fired did no damage. The British ships stayed for about a month in Tappan Bay (the Tappan Zee), north of the city, and then returned safely.

This small naval operation confirmed Washington's fears that his positions in New York were untenable. He had to hold Brooklyn Heights in order to hold Manhattan, for the heights dominated the defenses of the island. Yet he could not concentrate all his strength on the heights, because Manhattan was vulnerable from other directions also. Therefore he had to divide his limited forces. And now there was clear evidence that no matter what he did in Brooklyn and lower Manhattan, the British could make their way up the Hudson and land behind him, cutting off and destroying his army.

But Congress had ordered Washington to hold New York, and he himself realized the city's great strategic importance. He decided to try.

Preliminaries on Long Island

On August 22 a force of 15,000 British troops crossed the Narrows from Staten Island to Gravesend Bay, Long Island. The helpless American regiment guarding the landing area quickly withdrew. The leading British elements, under General Earl Charles Cornwallis, advanced north and took Flatbush. Two days later another 5,000 men arrived. These were soldiers from the German state of Hesse, under Major General Leopold von Heister; they had entered the service of the British Crown under a recent treaty.

Meanwhile General Greene, who had been in command of American forces on Long Island, became ill. He was replaced first by General Sullivan and then by General Putnam, who Washington thought was better qualified to carry out a determined defense. Sullivan remained in command of Greene's division.

Putnam's command, about 10,000 troops, was based on the fortified area of Brooklyn Heights, in the northwestern corner of Long Island. About half of the force, under Sullivan's command, was deployed on Long Island Heights, to cover the approaches to the fortifications. Long Island Heights was a long east-west ridge separating the southern flatlands, now held by the British, from the northern part of the island. The two main passes across Long Island Heights—Flatbush Pass and Bedford Pass—were strongly held and a line of outposts protected the ridgeline. Far to the east was Jamaica Pass, which was kept under observation by a mounted patrol.

The first hint of a British assault came at about 1:00 A.M. of August 27, at the Red Lion Inn, near Gowanus Bay. This was the extreme right of the American lines, held by troops under Brigadier General William Alexander (known as Lord Stirling). As some British troops under Major General James Grant approached, American outposts opened fire. Putnam was informed of the fire fight, and wakened Stirling, ordering him to deal with the British threat. This was apparently the only positive action taken that day by General Putnam.

By 3:00 A.M. Stirling was advancing with his brigade to join his threatened outposts. He deployed his Maryland and Delaware troops east of Gowanus Bay. As more British troops came up, the firing intensified, but the British seemed to be deterred by the American alertness.

At the same time as the activity near Red Lion Inn, General von Heister's Hessian artillery opened fire on the Flatbush and Bedford passes. General Sullivan assumed personal command at Flatbush Pass about 8:00 A.M. The Hessian artillery continued firing, but no infantry attack came. Sullivan learned from a messenger that the same was true at Bedford Pass.

Far to the east, northwest of Jamaica Pass, lay the Pennsylvania regiment of Colonel Samuel Miles. It is not clear whether Miles had been given responsibility for guarding the pass, but in any event, at about 7:00 A.M. he decided to check on the

31

situation there. At 8:00 A.M., Miles and his 500 men marched unexpectedly into the midst of a mass of British troops, advancing rapidly westward from Jamaica Pass. It was Howe's main body, 10,000 strong.

The British Envelopment

At 9:00 the night before, following a well-conceived plan, the British main force had secretly moved out from Flatland toward Jamaica Pass. They were guided by three local Loyalist farmers. The attack near Red Lion Inn and the Hessians' artillery bombardments were diversions. The main force swept easily through Jamaica Pass, capturing a five-man cavalry patrol before anyone could even fire a shot to give warning.

Miles and his men did put up a brief fight, but the noise was muffled by trees and hills, and no word of the action reached General Putnam or any other senior American officer. A few of Miles's men who were on horseback escaped, however, and galloped to Brooklyn Heights, where they informed Putnam. He inexplicably took no action and did not inform his subordinates.

Sullivan's first warning came at 9:00 A.M., when he heard two guns fired behind him. It was General Sir Henry Clinton at Bedford, leading the forward element of the enveloping British force. He had fired the two guns as a signal to von Heister, and to Grant near the Red Lion Inn. Sullivan immediately rushed a regiment toward Bedford, but it was thrown back by Clinton's advancing troops. At the same time, von Heister responded to Clinton's signal by smashing through Flatbush Pass with a

32

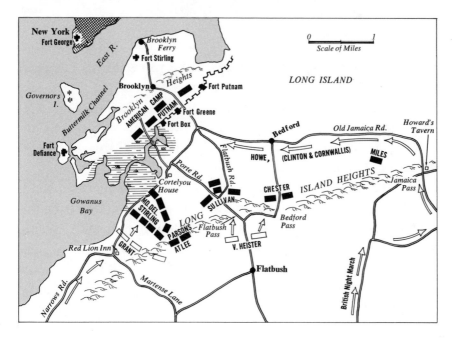

Battle of Long Island.

bayonet attack. Sullivan, hopelessly trapped between two fires, was captured along with several hundred of his surviving men.

Grant could not make his attack simultaneously with von Heister's, because he was waiting for ammunition to replenish what he had used up in the early morning diversion. It came at 10:00 A.M., along with 2,000 Royal Marines, increasing Grant's force to 7,000 men.

At first Stirling's brigade of 1,500 stopped the British attack. Then Stirling heard firing to his left rear, and realized that the British were behind him and his retreat was cut off. The supposedly impassable Gowanus Marsh was to his right rear. Stirling, however, had seen some of his men carrying wounded back along a trail through the marsh, and he decided that it had to

33

be tried. But first he had to hold off the threat to his left rear. Ordering two of his regiments to retire slowly before Grant and to work their way back through the marsh, Stirling took 500 Maryland Continental troops under Colonel William Smallwood and launched a counterattack against Cornwallis, who was approaching from Bedford.

General Washington, who had arrived at Sullivan's headquarters about 9:00 A.M., was now observing the action from the high ground inside the fortifications of Brooklyn Heights. Seeing what Stirling was doing, he quickly sent a detachment to help cover the withdrawal across Gowanus Marsh. Stirling himself and Smallwood's men, after charging five times, were finally surrounded and captured. "Good God, what brave men must I lose this day!" Washington is reported to have exclaimed as he watched Stirling's attacks.

Washington's Decision

It was now about noon; the battle was over, and the surviving Americans had retreated into the Brooklyn Heights fortifications. Washington had crucial decisions ahead. He expected the British to assault Brooklyn Heights that afternoon; if they succeeded 10,000 men would be lost—half of his entire New York army. Yet there was no time to organize an evacuation across the East River. He decided to hold at all costs, and sent for reinforcements. He doubted if Brooklyn Heights could be held for long. But it must be held long enough to permit a deliberate decision.

Howe had made his own decision, meanwhile, and had

34

chosen not to assault the fortifications. He remembered the terrible losses his troops had suffered at Bunker Hill in attacking an American fortified position. Siege operations would be slower, but safer and surer, he felt. During the night of August 27–28 the British began digging parallel and approach trenches as the first step in the eighteenth-century procedure for taking a fortified position by siege.

When Washington saw the trenches on the morning of August 28, he realized that he would not have to meet a frontal assault in the manner of Bunker Hill. Instead there would be a systematic hammering by British siege artillery and finally a well-prepared attack by greatly superior forces. Admiral Howe could send men up the Hudson to land behind him, as Washington had known all along. And the admiral's naval guns could be used along with General Howe's siege guns to batter the Brooklyn fortifications. As Washington had probably realized earlier, Brooklyn Heights could not be held for long. He must withdraw from Brooklyn.

The withdrawal had to be carried out without the knowledge of the British, or else the American force—now about three-fifths of Washington's army—would surely be destroyed. Knowing that there were Loyalist spies all around him, Washington made his plans but did not tell anyone of his decision until late in the afternoon of August 29. Then he told his senior officers that the evacuation would take place that same night.

The Evacuation

A picked force of about 2,000 men, including the survivors of Smallwood's Maryland regiment, was placed under command of Brigadier General Thomas Mifflin and ordered to hold the fortifications until every other man had embarked for Manhattan. The other troops were told that reinforcements from Manhattan were relieving them, and that they should withdraw and embark. The operation began at dark. It was jeopardized by a mistaken order to Mifflin to withdraw before the main body of troops was embarked, but the blunder was corrected before the British discovered that the fortifications were unmanned. At 4:00 A.M., Mifflin's men left their positions for the last time and embarked as the early dawn was breaking.

It was about 4:30 when the British discovered that the American trenches were empty. Pushing forward cautiously, they reached the river a little before 7:00 A.M., just as the last American boat was pulling away from the Brooklyn shore. Washington had been the last man to climb into that last boat, so it was especially fortunate for the American cause that the hasty British fire did it no damage.

The Americans had lost about 1,500 men in the Battle of Long Island, 1,100 of them captured. The British had lost about 300 killed and wounded, plus 23 captured by Stirling's men.

Washington had made many mistakes. He had attempted to hold an untenable position, and had placed undue confidence in General Putnam, who was a loyal and patriotic inspirer of men but no commander or tactician. Washington had also failed to protect his plans and dispositions from the spies who were so

36

Retreat from Long Island, August 30, 1776. Three days after the disastrous defeat by General Howe's British, Washington saved his army by a brilliantly planned and executed withdrawal across the East River to Manhattan. (Charles Phelps Cushing)

numerous in Loyalist-inclined New York. He had waited too long before taking personal command of the forces on Long Island.

Washington, however, had the priceless ability to learn from his mistakes. The sound decision on the twenty-seventh to reinforce his panic-stricken men, the sound decision on the twenty-eighth to evacuate, and the flawless way in which the evacuation was planned and carried out on the twenty-ninth—all showed how quickly he could learn.

37

CHAPTER 4

Trenton–Princeton

Defeat and Retreat

In the three months after the Battle of Long Island, superior British strength and skill drove the Americans out of New York, off Manhattan Island, across the Hudson River, and into central New Jersey. There had been few bright spots for Washington in this grim period of defeat and disappointment. But he had at least learned the limitations of his troops, and what units and what men could be relied upon in emergency and in adversity. And he had gained invaluable command and leadership experience himself, which could prove useful later in the war.

But as his ragged, dwindling, discouraged army retreated across New Jersey, Washington had serious doubts that the war could last much longer. Close behind him was a large British force under Lord Cornwallis. It would be suicidal to stand and fight against the much larger force of well-trained British regulars. If Washington's army were to be destroyed, he knew that the Revolutionary cause would be destroyed with it.

As he retreated toward the bridgeless Delaware River, Washington ordered that the New Jersey bank of the river be swept clear of all boats. Those that were not needed to transport his pathetic little army across the river were to be moved to the

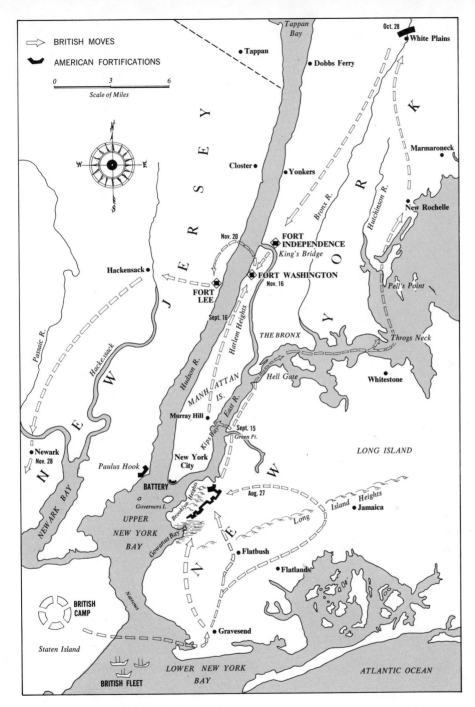

BRITISH MOVES

AMERICAN FORTIFICATIONS

0   3   6
Scale of Miles

Tappan Bay

Oct. 28
White Plains

• Tappan

• Dobbs Ferry

J E R S E Y

Closter •

• Yonkers

Marmaroneck •

• New Rochelle

Hutchinson R.

Bronx R.

Nov. 20

FORT
INDEPENDENCE
King's Bridge

Hackensack •

FORT
LEE

FORT WASHINGTON
Nov. 16

Sept. 16

Pell's Point

THE BRONX

Throgs Neck

Passaic R.

Hackensack

Hudson R.

Harlem Heights

Hell Gate

Whitestone •

N E W

MANHATTAN IS.

East R.

Murray Hill •

Kips Bay

Sept. 15
Green Pt.

LONG ISLAND

• Newark
Nov. 28

Paulus Hook

New York
City

BATTERY

Governors I.

Brooklyn Heights

Aug. 27

Long Island Heights

• Jamaica

UPPER
NEW YORK
BAY

Gowanus Bay

N E W

• Flatbush

• Flatlands

NEWARK BAY

BRITISH
CAMP

Narrows

• Gravesend

Staten Island

BRITISH FLEET

LOWER NEW YORK
BAY

ATLANTIC OCEAN

Operations around New York, 1776.

Pennsylvania shore. The crossing was completed at Trenton on December 8, just as Cornwallis and the leading British troops marched into the town.

Discovering that there were no boats available to continue the pursuit, Cornwallis decided to rest his tired troops. He sent a report to Howe, who was still in New York, that the Americans had escaped. Howe decided to put his army into winter quarters, and to wait until spring before destroying Washington and his surviving troops.

By December 20, 1776, Washington had received some reinforcements and was encamped with the main body of his army, about 2,500 men, between Taylorsville and Yardleyville, in Pennsylvania, just west of the Delaware River. Colonel John Cadwalader had slightly more than 2,000 Pennsylvania militiamen and Continentals near Bristol, and Brigadier General James Ewing had fewer than 1,000 at the river bend near Bordentown. There were a few other smaller units, making a total of 7,600 men on paper, but less than 6,000 effectives.

Washington knew that the chief danger was no longer that of an immediate attack by the British. They could afford to stay in bivouac through the winter and finish off the Americans in better weather. The real threat now was the imminent disintegration of the army. Only half the men Washington now had were veterans of earlier fighting; the rest were raw recruits. Most of the veterans would be with him only a few more days, since their enlistments ran out at the end of the year. The men were dressed in rags, many were without shoes, and repeated defeats and withdrawals had drained them of hope.

A Daring Plan

In this dismal situation, Washington's considered remedy was a daring aggressive move. To cross the Delaware and strike the British by surprise seemed to offer the only chance of holding the army together. He knew he was risking disaster, but disaster was certain if he did nothing.

Washington had made his decision by December 23. That day he issued orders that three days' rations be cooked, and ammunition and flints were distributed to the troops. The next day he announced his plans to his commanders. He would attack Trenton, which was garrisoned by a brigade of Hessians.

The move would come on Christmas night. Washington would lead the main force of 2,400 Continentals across the river at McKonkey's Ferry, 9 miles north of Trenton, and strike the town at dawn. General Ewing would cross just south of Trenton, with about 800 Pennsylvania and New Jersey militia, and seize the bridge across Assunpink Creek, so as to keep the British and Hessians from withdrawing south toward Bordentown. Cadwalader was to take his force across near Bristol and make diversionary attacks on the British and Hessian troops at Mount Holly and Bordentown, keeping them occupied so they would not fall on Washington at Trenton.

The River Crossing

The little army assembled about 3:00 P.M. on Christmas afternoon, and Washington saw that few men had overcoats, and that many lacked shoes. It was getting dark as they reached the

Crossing the Delaware River to Trenton, December 25–26, 1776. This was the beginning of Washington's brilliant campaign that transformed his defeated soldiers into a victorious army, and that saved the Revolution. (Perry Pictures)

ferry, at about 5:00. Snow was beginning to fall and the breeze freshened. The snow continued and the wind rose to gale force as the men were ferried across in the sturdy, 50-foot Durham boats Washington had taken earlier from the Jersey shore.

Things went much more slowly than Washington had expected. Stiff, frozen fingers could not work well; everything was icy and slippery, making it difficult for men to pick things up and to carry them. Loading and unloading heavy guns and

42

frightened horses was particularly difficult. And each crossing was hindered by chunks of ice in the swift-flowing Delaware. To make things worse, at 11:00 P.M. the snow turned to sleet. The crossing was finally completed by 3:00 A.M., three hours later than Washington had planned. The army was soon on the march toward Trenton.

The force divided at the Birmingham crossroads. Greene's division was to move on Trenton from the northwest by the Pennington Road, while Sullivan's stayed on the River Road. Washington accompanied Greene. At this point—about 5:30 A.M.—came more bad news. Sullivan sent a message that his men's muskets were too wet to fire. Since there could be no turning back, Washington barely hesitated before saying, "Tell General Sullivan to use the bayonet. I am resolved to take Trenton!"

Then came the news that a detachment of Brigadier General Adam Stephen's brigade had carried out a raid on Hessian outposts around Trenton during the night, probably ruining all chance of surprise. The captain in charge had gained Stephen's permission for the raid, but Stephen had not asked Washington's. Now openly furious, Washington sharply rebuked Stephen, expecting that the Hessians would be drawn up in formation waiting for him when he reached Trenton.

Despite the raid, and even though it was almost 8:00 A.M. and well after dawn when the Americans reached Trenton, the Hessians were unprepared. There had been much Christmas feasting by the troops, and partying late into the night by the officers. Because of the sleet storm, the usual morning patrols had been called off, and the sentries stood with their backs to the cold north wind and thus to the Americans.

43

The commander of the Hessian brigade holding the town was Colonel Johann Rall, a brave but somewhat careless officer. He had three regiments. One he commanded himself, one was under the command of a Colonel von Knyphausen, and one was under a Colonel von Lossberg.

The Battle of Trenton

Washington had apparently been able to keep in close touch with Sullivan. The Greene-Washington force attacked Trenton from the north at the same time Sullivan was striking from the west. The time was eight o'clock.

As the surprised Hessian sentries fell back firing, American artillery was hauled up and placed wheel to wheel at the head of the two main streets, King and Queen, which ran parallel to each other, north to south, through the town. Colonel Henry Knox's cannoneers had managed to keep the big guns dry and fit for firing. As the Hessians formed into detachments and began marching north and west to meet the Americans, the streets were swept by canister.*

Supported by Knox's artillery, Greene's men attacked from the north. Stephen's brigade pushed down King and Queen streets, Stirling and Brigadier General Hugh Mercer struck from the northwest, and the brigade of Brigadier General Roche de Fermoy, a French officer who had recently joined the Americans, blocked the road to Princeton east of the town. Two Hessian

* Small lead balls that broke out of their containing shell as soon as they were fired and scattered like buckshot.

44

cannon that were wheeled into King Street were almost immediately seized by a company of Stephen's Virginians under Captain William Washington and Lieutenant James Monroe. Sullivan's men attacked from the west along Front Street and soon blocked the bridge across the Assunpink Creek.

By now Washington realized that Ewing had not arrived south of the Assunpink. To prevent the Hessians from escaping, Washington shifted Stephen's and Fermoy's brigades to the east of the town, with Stirling moving to his left to continue the drive down King and Queen streets.

The trap at Trenton was closed. There was no way out for the Hessians. Colonel Rall led his regiment and the von Lossberg regiment in a counterattack, but he fell mortally wounded, and the regiments surrendered. The von Knyphausen regiment surrendered a few minutes later to General Sullivan, after vainly searching for a way across Assunpink Creek.

The battle had lasted a little over an hour. The Hessians lost 22 men killed, and 948 taken prisoner, including 92 wounded. About 430 escaped to spread the alarm. The Americans had lost two men who froze to death on the march to Trenton and four wounded in the battle. Most of the Hessian casualties were from artillery or bayonet; neither side was able to fire muskets effectively in the sleet. Gathering up their prisoners and much captured equipment, the Americans returned to McKonkey's Ferry, and by nightfall were back in their camps, exhausted but happy.

Washington had won a small victory—but it was a decisive and dramatic one. News of it soon spread the length of the new country, encouraging Patriot Americans from Congress to the

45

Princeton

Stony Brook

0   1   2
Scale of Miles

Stony Brook Bridge

Quaker Meeting House

Routes used by Cornwallis
in advance on Trenton
Jan. 2, 1777

Maidenhead
(Lawrenceville)

Turnpike (Post Road)

Washington's route to
Princeton Jan. 2-3., 1777

Old Road

Pennington

Assunpink Creek

Quaker Road

GREENE

Washington's route to
Trenton Dec. 25-26, 1776

Washington
Dec. 30-Jan. 2

Birmingham

Trenton

SULLIVAN

McKonkey's Ferry

Burlington

Delaware R.

Taylorsville

Trenton-Princeton Campaign, December, 1776–January, 1777.

newest volunteer in the army, and gaining surprised respect for Washington from the British. Most important, the victory at Trenton encouraged many of the army veterans to reenlist, and stimulated the recruitment of new men.

Back Across the River

Late on the twenty-seventh, Washington learned that Cadwalader, ashamed of his failure to contribute to his commander's victory, had earlier that day taken his 2,000 men across to the Jersey shore of the river. Finding that the Hessians had abandoned Bordentown, he sent a message to Washington urging the commander in chief to join him at Crosswicks, a few miles inland. Washington feared that if he ordered Cadwalader to return across the river, the psychological damage would offset the results of the victory of the twenty-sixth. He felt he had no choice but to take his tired men across the river for a third time. First he gave them a good, if belated, Christmas dinner on the twenty-seventh. Since Cadwalader was not in contact with the enemy and did not appear in immediate danger, Washington rested his men on December 28 and set out on the twenty-ninth with the 1,500 veterans who were well enough to make the journey.

Reoccupying Trenton, Washington established a defensive position south of the town, behind Assunpink Creek. He sent messages to Generals Heath at Peekskill and Alexander McDougall at Morristown to join him. During the last two days of the year, through personal pleas, Washington persuaded a majority of his men to reenlist. Then, on January 1, having

47

learned that General Cornwallis was at Princeton, Washington sent Fermoy's brigade to delay the British between Princeton and Trenton. Sullivan's division was placed in a delaying position in Trenton.

Cornwallis and the "Old Fox"

Promptly and vigorously, Cornwallis began his advance toward Trenton on the morning of January 2. He had a force of 8,000 British regulars. Fermoy inexplicably left his position and returned to Trenton, but Colonel Edward Hand took over command of the American delaying force and managed the troops well. He fell back slowly before the greatly superior British force. By midafternoon the British were within a mile of Trenton. Washington ordered Hand to withdraw from his last delaying position, just outside of Trenton, at 4:00 P.M. Hand's and Sullivan's men continued to delay the British in the town itself until dark.

Soon after dark the British reached the north bank of Assunpink Creek and could see the American trenches, lit by their campfires, on the south bank. Cornwallis decided to wait until daylight to attack, believing the Americans were hopelessly trapped between the Assunpink, the Delaware, and the sea to the southeast. He was persuaded by the brightness of their campfires and the noise of their entrenching operations that Washington's men were making desperate preparations for battle the next day. He told one of his officers: "We'll bag the old fox in the morning."

Cornwallis was awakened at dawn by the sound of distant

48

firing to his rear, at Princeton. The American positions south of Assunpink Creek were empty.

Now skilled in achieving surprise, Washington had sent his baggage trains to Burlington early in the evening, and set out with his men at midnight, in silence, for Princeton. He left a detachment at the Assunpink to keep the fires burning and to make noises as though digging in. The Americans took narrow back roads unknown to the British, and reached a stream called Stony Brook, 2 miles south of Princeton, just before dawn. They followed the road a mile farther, as it ran parallel to the brook, to the Quaker Meeting House. There the old road into Princeton turned sharply right. Half a mile north the new Post Road, Cornwallis' line of communications, ran into Princeton, parallel to the old road.

Washington sent General Mercer straight north with his brigade to destroy the Post Road bridge over Stony Brook. Mercer was then to block the Post Road so as to hold off Cornwallis if he returned from Trenton, and also keep the British in Princeton from escaping in that direction. The main body of Washington's army moved on along the old road toward Princeton.

The Battle of Princeton

Mercer soon ran into two British regiments, plus some cavalry —about 800 men in all. This was a force under Colonel Charles Mawhood, who was marching to join Cornwallis at Trenton. Mawhood's men were crossing the bridge just as Mercer's

49

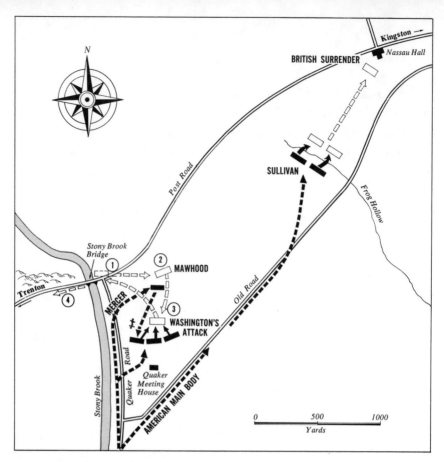

Battle of Princeton, January 3, 1777.

troops approached. Both Mercer and Mawhood quickly deployed their troops east of the brook.

Mawhood immediately attacked the smaller American force. Washington, hearing the firing, and seeing that Mercer was outnumbered, ordered Cadwalader and his 900 Pennsylvania militiamen to go to his aid. Cadwalader's men arrived just as Mercer's brigade was beginning a demoralized retreat; Mercer had been fatally wounded in a British bayonet charge. At the same time, however, two American guns in an orchard on the American right opened fire on Mawhood's force. Cadwalader's men started ahead confidently, then fled at the first British volley.

At this point, Washington himself took command of the engagement. He ordered Colonel Daniel Hitchcock's brigade of veteran New England Continentals into position on the right of Mercer's and Cadwalader's men, and personally rallied the panic-stricken militiamen. Then he rode toward the British, waving his men forward with his hat. Hitchcock enveloped the British left flank as Mercer's men turned their right. Mawhood had to force his way across the bridge with a bayonet charge to make good his retreat toward Trenton. An American cavalry charge, by the Philadelphia Light Horse, led by Washington himself, turned Mawhood's retreat into a rout.

After destroying the Stony Brook bridge, Washington turned toward the town of Princeton, where he found that Sullivan had already defeated a small force that Mawhood had left there to guard supplies. This British detachment had withdrawn into the grounds of Princeton College and nearly half of them had made Nassau Hall into an impromptu fort. But Captain Alexander Hamilton's artillery battery had fired into the building, and the British had soon surrendered.

The British lost about 100 killed and wounded, and 200 taken prisoner, while the Americans had about 40 killed and wounded. After his men had plundered the British supplies at Princeton, Washington got them on the road again. As frustrated Cornwallis was approaching Princeton from the south— to be delayed by the destroyed bridge at Stony Brook—the

Americans were safely on their way to the inland, mountainous region around Morristown.

The American Revolution had not died in that winter of 1776–77, as had seemed inevitable. Rather it had taken on new life and hope. The Americans now knew that they had a leader who was a match for the best British generals.

CHAPTER 5

Saratoga Campaign

The British Plan

The British had an ambitious plan recommended by General Burgoyne for northern operations in 1777. It called for converging attacks from three directions to meet at Albany, thus seizing control of the Hudson Valley and cutting New England off from the remainder of the rebellious colonies.

Burgoyne himself would lead the main attack, a drive south with 7,500 men up Lake Champlain and then down the Hudson to Albany. A smaller offensive, down the Mohawk Valley from Lake Ontario, would be commanded by Lieutenant Colonel Barry St. Leger, who was made a temporary brigadier general. The third of the converging drives was to be Howe's expected thrust up the Hudson from New York City. If Howe had not already reached Albany when Burgoyne's and St. Leger's men met there, the combined forces from the north would sweep down to make contact with Howe.

The plan had several serious flaws. To bring three separate forces over several hundred miles to converge at a given point required precise timing and coordination that would be extremely hard to achieve in wilderness country. The supply problems alone were overwhelming. Even more serious, General Howe's cooperation was never gained for the plan. Howe had, in fact, obtained approval from the British government for an entirely different plan—a thrust at Philadelphia that he hoped would crush Washington's army.

As it turned out, St. Leger was repulsed by Benedict Arnold when less than halfway to his destination. Howe moved southward to attack Philadelphia instead of northward. And although Burgoyne himself took Fort Ticonderoga, and his troops won a minor victory at Hubbardtown, he suffered a serious setback at Bennington, losing a considerable portion of his German troops. In early September he was at Fort Edward on the east bank of the Hudson. His army, now about 6,000 strong, was dependent on a tenuous supply line stretching back to Montreal, with winter approaching.

Burgoyne could have returned to Canada, but he was determined to push ahead with the plan that he himself had conceived. He could have moved down the east bank of the Hudson, where there were no American forces, but Albany, his destination, was on the west bank. Burgoyne knew that sooner or later he would have to cross the river and face General Horatio Gates, who lay on that western bank somewhere above Albany. Burgoyne chose, therefore, to cross at Fort Edward, march south, and try to defeat Gates wherever he found him. With only thirty days' rations and supplies, he had to get to Albany or lose his army. He could not live through the winter on the rations he had, nor hope to be supplied from Canada during the winter.

Burgoyne discovered Gates between Saratoga (now Schuyler-ville) and Stillwater, entrenched on Bemis Heights beside the Hudson. Gates had 7,000 men, including the Virginia and Pennsylvania riflemen of Colonel Daniel Morgan's corps. These were veteran Continental fighters and skilled marksmen.

Looking north from Bemis Heights, there were several significant landmarks. First came Mill Creek, cutting through the wooded plateau to flow into the Hudson. Beyond it was a 15-acre cleared area known as Freeman's Farm, and beyond that a long east-west depression called the Great Ravine. Burgoyne's headquarters was several miles farther north, just below Saratoga.

Burgoyne's Indian scouts had by now deserted, and he had only the roughest knowledge of Gates's positions. So on September 19, 1777, he planned to make an attack that was really a reconnaissance in force. If the situation was favorable, he intended to envelop the American left and drive Gates into the river. Brigadier General Simon Fraser's advanced corps, reinforced by Colonel Heinrich C. Breymann's Germans, would make the main effort, circling wide to the west and striking for unfortified high ground which Burgoyne knew was just northwest of the American fortifications. Fraser had 2,000 men in all. Far to the east, capable General Baron Friedrich A. von Riedesel, commander of Burgoyne's Brunswick (German) division, would lead 1,100 men of three Brunswick regiments, along with eight guns, taking a road that hugged the river. Burgoyne himself would accompany a force between these two wings, making a secondary effort against the center of the

American front. This force would be made up of Brigadier General Hamilton's 1,100-man brigade with its six guns.

The British operation required the concentration on the battlefield of three widely separated forces, but Burgoyne intended to assure coordination by signal guns, which he would direct personally. The concentrated forces would be far outnumbered by the American defenders, but Burgoyne had no way of knowing American strength. Furthermore, part of his objective was to gain information about the Americans, if the attack should not gain an immediate victory.

The British moved out on the morning of September 19. Fraser marched straight west, beyond the head of the Great Ravine, and then turned south toward Freeman's Farm. Burgoyne and Hamilton crossed the Great Ravine and deployed in the Freeman's Farm clearing. The third column, von Reidesel's, made slow progress along the river road, delayed by broken bridges over minor tributaries.

In the American camp there was increasing tension between Gates and his principal subordinate, Brigadier General Benedict Arnold, who commanded the left wing. Gates was a shrewd manipulator and overcautious commander; Arnold, an excellent aggressive tactician, and a daring, inspiring battlefield leader. When the British were sighted, Arnold urged going to meet them, while Gates insisted on staying put behind the fortifications. Finally, about 1:00 P.M., he agreed to let Arnold send Morgan and his riflemen out to protect the American left and to learn something of British intentions.

Morgan's men swept quickly but cautiously through the woods, finding a few Canadians, Tories, and Indians just south of Freeman's Farm. They shot down most of them, and pursued

56

the survivors right into Hamilton's right regiment, drawn up in formation in the Freeman's Farm clearing. The Virginians were startled and thrown back by a volley from the British. Morgan rallied them as Arnold pushed in two New Hampshire regiments of Enoch Poor's New York and New Hampshire brigade on Morgan's left. These were soon engaged and thrown back by Fraser's men, but Arnold had found a gap between Fraser and Hamilton, and he hastened to exploit it. Throwing the rest of Poor's brigade into the gap, he forced Hamilton to swing westward, just as his center was pushing forward in response to Burgoyne's gun signal for a general advance. Thus Hamilton's line was weakened close to the breaking point.

The British guns never got into action; American sharpshooters picked the crews off as fast as they were replaced. The battle raged all afternoon, with Arnold's division fighting alone while Gates kept the rest of the big American force within the fortifications.

Arnold, sure he could break through the British line with a few more troops, dashed back to demand reinforcements. Gates refused. Finally Gates sent out General Ebenezer Learned's brigade, but he pettily refused to let Arnold accompany him, or to return to the battlefield at all. Learned went too far west, missed the weakened area of the British line, and was thrown back by Fraser's grenadiers and light infantry.

General von Riedesel was the hero of the day for the British cause. Still pushing down the river road, he heard Burgoyne's gun signal for the general advance. He also heard the firing of Arnold's fight on the British right, and began moving toward it. When Burgoyne sent to him for guns, he dispatched them promptly over trails he had already reconnoitered. When Bur-

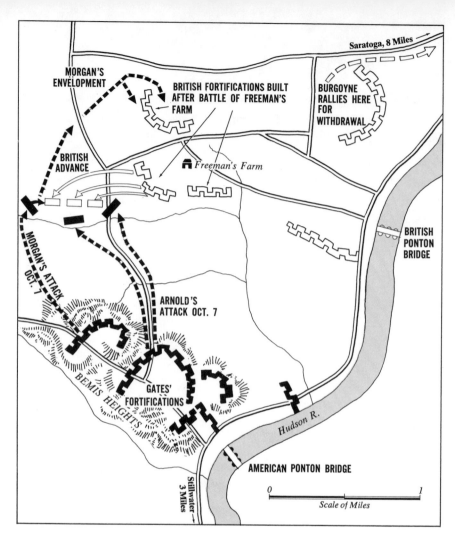

Battle of Saratoga.

goyne then sent for men, at five o'clock, Riedesel moved out immediately, leading the way himself. Arriving on the battlefield and taking in the situation immediately, Riedesel threw his men in against Arnold's right flank as fast as they came up, repulsing the surprised Americans. The Brunswick guns arrived at the same time and began pouring grapeshot into the American ranks. The German infantry fired a volley, and the Americans withdrew, ending the battle.

The Americans had lost 65 men killed, 218 wounded, and 33 missing. British losses had been shockingly high: about 600 killed, wounded, or captured out of fewer than 1,000 men continuously engaged. The Americans had conducted a highly successful defense, thanks to Arnold and his men, but a great opportunity to defeat Burgoyne decisively had been missed through Gates's overcaution.

One aftermath of the battle was a climax in the hostility between Gates and Arnold. Jealous of the praise given Arnold by his fellow officers, Gates deliberately omitted any mention of his fiery subordinate from his official report on the battle. After several bitter arguments and an exchange of insulting letters, he relieved Arnold of command, appointed Major General Benjamin Lincoln in his place, and barred him from headquarters. Arnold prepared to leave, but the other general officers urged him to stay, and he did, with Gates's permission but without any command.

Battle of Bemis Heights

Burgoyne had different problems. He now had barely 5,000 effective men, and a poorer chance of defeating Gates, who was receiving reinforcements every day. Yet Burgoyne had some hope that Sir Henry Clinton, who was operating in the Hudson Highlands area south of Albany, would be able to sail up and help him. With his men on short rations and his horses dying for lack of feed, Burgoyne decided on another reconnaissance in force to test the American left. If the Americans were too strong, the British would withdraw, reopen their line of communications northward, and wait for Sir Henry Clinton. The probing attack was set for October 7.

On that morning the British and Germans moved out, with no specified objective, but rather the intention of feeling out American strength. The Americans had now fortified the high ground that had been General Fraser's objective in the Freeman's Farm battle. The British had built earthwork fortifications of their own on the Freeman's Farm clearing.

Fraser advanced on the right with Major Earl Alexander Balcarres' light infantry. Riedesel led the center column, which included the 24th Foot regiment of Fraser's corps and some Brunswick units. Major John Dyke Acland was on the left with his grenadier battalion, also detached from Fraser's corps.

As the British approached, Morgan urged Gates to attack Burgoyne's right. Gates characteristically held back, despite his greatly superior numbers. Finally he sent Morgan's brigade against the British right and Poor's brigade against the left. Later he sent Learned's brigade against the British center. Three-fourths of his army of 11,000 men remained in the fortifications.

Poor's 800 men moved out immediately and hit the British left at 2:30 P.M. Overwhelming the British by superior numbers, the Americans rolled up the left, capturing the wounded Acland. Morgan then hit the right flank, pushing it back and leaving Riedesel, in the center, unprotected. At this point, Benedict Arnold, defying Gates, rode into battle on his big bay horse. He took command, pushing Learned's men forward

60

against the center. When the attack was repulsed, Arnold led them forward again, and the British began withdrawing into their earthworks. General Fraser tried to rally them, and was mortally wounded by one of Morgan's riflemen.

Although Gates had apparently ordered no general attack, his whole army now took to the field, joining the attack. Arnold led Learned's brigade against the British horseshoe redoubt at the western end of the Great Ravine. Morgan, Poor, and Learned surrounded the redoubt and Arnold led the assault, until his leg was broken by a bullet that knocked him from his horse. But the redoubt was taken; its commander, Breymann, was killed in the desperate struggle.

This ended the Second Battle of Saratoga, also known as the Battle of Bemis Heights or the Battle of Stillwater. The British had lost 600 men killed, wounded, or captured, plus ten guns, while the Americans had lost a total of about 150 men. Burgoyne pulled back north of the Great Ravine during the night, and the next day started on a slow withdrawal to Saratoga. Gates pursued, and sent a flanking force up the east bank of the Hudson.

On October 12, almost surrounded, Burgoyne decided, at Riedesel's suggestion, to slip back to Fort Edward and Lake George, abandoning all baggage and artillery. Before the march began, however, a new American force arrived to complete the encirclement. A few days earlier John Stark of New Hampshire, bitter at shabby treatment by Congress, had marched his 1,100 militiamen away from Bemis Heights the day their enlistments expired. But he had second thoughts, and now he was back, just in time to seal the British in and share the glory of the Saratoga victory.

61

Surrender of Burgoyne, October 17, 1777. Isolated in the wilderness of northern New York, after his defeats at Saratoga on September 19 and October 7, Burgoyne had no choice but to surrender. General Horatio Gates, who received Burgoyne's surrender, got the credit for the victories, which had actually been won by Benedict Arnold (probably the officer shown leaning on the cannon, extreme right) and Daniel Morgan (in white leather frontiersman's shirt). Washington's strategy, and his assignment of his best troops and officers to Gates's command, was responsible for victory. (Charles Phelps Cushing)

Burgoyne asked for a parley on October 13, and on the seventeenth his army laid down its arms. The Americans captured 5,700 prisoners, including seven generals, and also 27 guns, 5,000 small arms, and much other matériel. Burgoyne's ambitious invasion had ended in disaster. All British posts to the north were withdrawn into Canada. The British now held only the New York City area, Rhode Island, and Philadelphia, which Howe had captured in September. Psychologically, Saratoga more than made up for the discouraging defeats around Philadelphia. In every way it was the unquestioned turning point of the Revolution.

Gates received popular credit for the victory at the time. It strengthened his already formidable position with Congress, and thus paved the way for later disasters. In fact, however, Arnold was the real victor on the battlefield, while strategically Saratoga was the fruit of Washington's sound grasp of the British plans and of his courage and skill in dealing with them. Recognizing that Burgoyne's advance was the most dangerous of the three British thrusts, he deliberately weakened his own forces, sending Gates the resources without which Saratoga could not have been won. These included Arnold, Daniel Morgan, and Morgan's 500 riflemen. All the while, Washington skillfully maneuvered to keep his own little army between Howe and Albany and yet to avoid battle with Howe. The Saratoga campaign was proof that Washington had become a great general.

CHAPTER 6

Brandywine

General Howe and Washington's Strategy

In December of 1776, when Washington had made his bold crossing of the Delaware, the British controlled central New Jersey right up to the river. Six months later, thanks to Washington's victories at Trenton and Princeton and his continued aggressive harassment of the enemy, there were no major British forces left in New Jersey.

Washington knew that British General Burgoyne was pushing south through Lake Champlain, and when General Howe pulled his men out of New Jersey in late June, 1777, Washington at first thought Howe planned to advance up the Hudson and join Burgoyne. When the British force put out to sea instead, Washington could only guess where it might strike. British control of the sea gave his enemy a tremendous advantage that Washington fully recognized.

General Howe's destination turned out to be the mouth of the Chesapeake Bay, and thence up the bay and the Elk River to its source at Head of Elk. There he would be in position to attack Philadelphia from the south. Howe had decided that the way to defeat the Americans was to destroy Washington's army. He knew the commander in chief would have to stand

and fight to protect the seat of Congress, and he believed he could destroy the army and seize the rebel capital in one campaign. Sixteen warships escorted 245 transports and supply ships, and there were 16,000 men in the invading force.

When Howe sailed from New York, Washington realized that his objective might be Philadelphia, and pressure from Congress led him to shift his army to central New Jersey so as to be able to move quickly to defend the capital if need be. Yet he could not believe that Howe would go away and leave Burgoyne unsupported and isolated in upper New York State.

Until Howe actually made his way into Chesapeake Bay, Washington felt he was probably feinting to the south and would reappear at New York to support Burgoyne. Meanwhile, as Burgoyne advanced farther and farther into upper New York, Washington detached some of his most reliable troops and most capable commanders to reinforce the Northern Army, and thus prevent Burgoyne from reaching Albany. He could ill afford to detach units like Morgan's rifle brigade, and commanders like Generals Arnold and Lincoln, but he knew that Burgoyne must be stopped at all costs. Furthermore, the opportunity to destroy a British army that was inland and isolated from British sea power was worth risking a defeat near the Atlantic coast.

Opposing Plans

Once Howe's intentions were clear, Washington had ample time to move southward from his camp on the Neshaminy River and take up defensive positions to protect Philadelphia. By

65

September 1 he had about 15,000 men, but more than one-third of these were unreliable militiamen. The Continental troops who made up the rest were organized in five divisions, commanded by Generals Greene, Sullivan, Stephen, Stirling, and William Maxwell.

Washington decided that the best defensive position was behind Brandywine Creek, which ran just north of Wilmington, a few miles before it poured into the Delaware River. Howe's natural route to Philadelphia would lead him to cross Chad's Ford (now Chadds Ford) on the Brandywine. The creek valley was deep and narrow, and made a defensible obstacle, although the stream was fordable in several places.

Washington posted Greene's division and Brigadier General Anthony Wayne's brigade of Maxwell's division at Chad's Ford. Farther south Brigadier General John Armstrong's Pennsylvania militia held the easily defended rugged cliffs overlooking Pyle's Ford. Sullivan's division was deployed to the north between Brinton's and Jones' fords, and was responsible for protecting the army's right flank. Sullivan had Colonel Moses Hazen and his regiment cover Wister's and Buffington's fords, still farther north. Stephen's and Stirling's divisions lay in reserve behind the Chad's Ford position.

Covering the expected British route toward Brandywine Creek was Maxwell's light infantry brigade, on the main road, and Colonel Theodorick Bland's 1st Dragoons, stationed west of Jones' Ford and responsible for screening all of the northern approaches to the creek up to Buffington's Ford. A Major Spear, with a body of Pennsylvania militia, had responsibility for security north of Buffington's Ford on the west side of the creek.

66

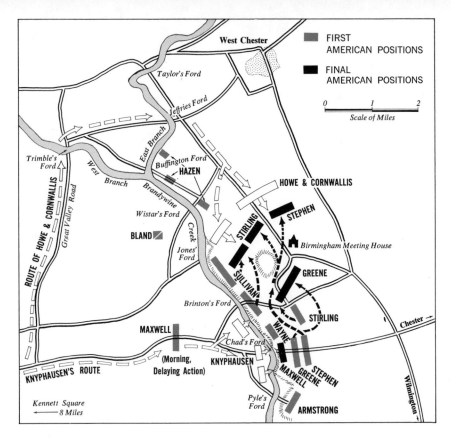

West Chester

Taylor's Ford

Jeffries Ford

East Branch

Trimble's Ford

Buffington Ford

HAZEN

West Branch

Brandywine

HOWE & CORNWALLIS

ROUTE OF HOWE & CORNWALLIS

Great Valley Road

Wistar's Ford

STIRLING

STEPHEN

Creek

BLAND

Birmingham Meeting House

Jones' Ford

SULLIVAN

GREENE

Brinton's Ford

STIRLING

Chester →

MAXWELL

WAYNE

Chad's Ford

(Morning,
Delaying Action)

KNYPHAUSEN

STEPHEN

KNYPHAUSEN'S ROUTE

MAXWELL

GREENE

Wilmington

Kennett Square
8 Miles

Pyle's
Ford

ARMSTRONG

0   1   2

Scale of Miles

Battle of the Brandywine, September 11, 1777.

Washington had been told that there were no more fords for twelve miles north of Buffington's. He did not reconnoiter the area himself, or have a trustworthy officer to do the job. His information was wrong. There was a good road, the Great Valley Road, that cut north from the main road well out of sight of his delaying positions. It then swung east, crossing both the West Branch and East Branch of the Brandywine before they joined just south of Buffington's Ford. Washington knew nothing of these crossings, but Howe and his corps command-

67

ers, Cornwallis and General William von Knyphausen, had carefully explored the area with the aid of local Loyalists. They knew the American dispositions and they knew of the open road to the north. Howe decided on the strategy that had worked so well at the Battle of Long Island—a frontal diversion, with a wide-sweeping envelopment as the main attack. Knyphausen, with 5,000 men, would make the frontal diversion; Cornwallis, with 8,000, would make the main attack.

The Opening Moves

The British moved out at dawn on September 11. Knyphausen's troops struck Maxwell's brigade about three miles from Chad's Ford. Maxwell fought a delaying action, slowly withdrawing, and two hours later brought his men across the creek and into position between Wayne's brigade and Greene's division. Knyphausen deployed his men on the west bank of the valley, between Chad's and Brinton's fords. He kept up an exchange of fire with the Americans that was just lively enough to hold their attention, and to cause them to expect a frontal attack across the creek. Cornwallis and his men were meanwhile making the long march along the Great Valley Road.

At about 11:00 A.M., Washington received a report from Colonel Hazen, through Sullivan, that there was a large body of British moving north of the Great Valley Road. Washington immediately sent a message to Colonel Bland, stationed west of the creek, ordering him to investigate. The reply from Bland was vague and unsatisfactory, but meanwhile Washington had received a very clear report from Lieutenant Colonel

68

James Ross, who apparently had been scouting in the enemy rear. Ross said that at 11:00 A.M. he had seen about 5,000 of the enemy, with 16 or 18 guns, on the Great Valley Road.

Washington was now convinced that Howe had divided his army, and he believed this would give the Americans a chance to defeat the British in detail. Washington ordered a counterattack across the Brandywine by Greene, Wayne, Maxwell, and Sullivan. Stirling and Stephen were to remain in reserve, between Chad's Ford and Birmingham Meeting House, about two miles behind the creek.

Then, just as the counterattacking force was beginning to move, Sullivan sent a third report, this one from Major Spear, stating that no British had been seen near the northern fords. Sullivan commented that the other two reports were probably wrong.

At about the same time, a little after 2:00 P.M., an excited local farmer ran into Washington's headquarters claiming that the British had crossed the Brandywine and were marching south toward Birmingham Meeting House. Washington could not believe that the enemy had gotten so far but, fortunately for the American cause, he called off his counterattack.

The British Envelopment

Another message soon confirmed the farmer's report, and Washington immediately deployed his troops for defense against the enveloping attack. He ordered Sullivan to swing his division into a new position facing north, at right angles to the line of the Brandywine. Stirling and Stephen were ordered to move to the right of Sullivan's new position, near Birmingham Meeting House. Sullivan was put in overall command of this new right wing.

Soon after he had made these arrangements, between 4:00 and 4:30, Washington heard heavy artillery and musket fire from the right rear, and realized that the British attack was in great force. He then pulled Greene back from Chad's Ford, leaving only Wayne's and Maxwell's brigades to hold the ford. Accompanying Greene, Washington hastened to the sound of the battle. He intended to place Greene's division well behind the three front divisions, southwest of the Birmingham Meeting House.

Sullivan, Stephen, and Stirling had been still deploying into their new positions when the British struck. Sullivan's division was hit hard, and after a brief, intense fight, gave way. Just at this point, Brigadier General George Weedon's Virginia brigade, of Greene's division, came up on the American left, and was able to hold the threatened position. Sullivan's men fell back through Weedon's ranks. Stephen's and Stirling's divisions held fast, and Cornwallis decided to stop for the night. The day had been hot, and his men were exhausted after their 16-mile march and 2-hour fight.

At Chad's Ford, meanwhile, Knyphausen had not been slow to take advantage of the removal of Greene's division. Under an intense artillery bombardment his troops crossed the creek valley and gained the east bank. Wayne and Maxwell delayed the Hessians, slowly withdrawing their badly outnumbered men in good order, although eight guns were lost.

Washington pulled his army back to Chester under cover of darkness. The Battle of the Brandywine had been an American defeat, largely because of Washington's failure to have the countryside properly reconnoitered. He had fought the battle skillfully, however, once the true tactical situation became clear, and the morale of the American troops remained good. They knew they had fought well, and thought they had inflicted heavier casualties than they had suffered. In reality, the Americans lost about 200 killed, 700 or 800 wounded, and almost 400 prisoners. British casualties were reported as 89 killed, 488 wounded, and 6 missing.

CHAPTER 7

Philadelphia and Germantown

An Ambitious Plan

Washington and General Howe spent the last half of September, 1777, maneuvering south of Philadelphia. Washington hoped to defeat Howe as he crossed the Schuylkill River. But the Americans were misled by a British feint. On September 26 the redcoats crossed the Schuylkill and marched easily into the American capital. Congress and a large number of citizens had left in panic a week earlier.

General Cornwallis and about 3,000 British troops settled down in Philadelphia, while the main body, 8,000 men, bivouacked at Germantown, about 5 miles northwest of the city. Howe prepared no defensive fortifications, and Washington, who knew the area well, saw an opportunity for a decisive surprise attack. He now had about 11,000 men in his constantly fluctuating army—8,000 Continentals and 3,000 militia. Thus he knew that he outnumbered the Germantown contingent of Howe's divided force.

Washington and his staff planned a night march ending in a surprise attack early on September 8. The plan was complicated, calling for the coordination of four separate columns marching in the dark.

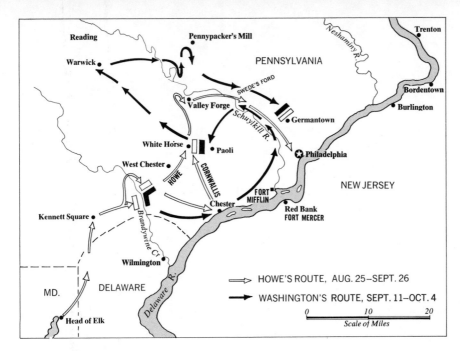

The Philadelphia Campaign.

On the far right, Brigadier General John Armstrong's Pennsylvania militia moved along the Manawatamy Road, and was to turn the British left flank. To Armstrong's left, along the main north-south road into Germantown, came General Sullivan, commanding his division and Wayne's brigade, making up the right-center of the American army. Washington accompanied Sullivan.

The main attack would be made by the American left-center under General Greene, commanding his own division and that of General Stephen, plus Brigadier General Alexander McDougall's brigade. Greene's force took the road from Bethlehem to an intersection several miles north of Chestnut Hill. Then he took a road that ran southeast to a point almost due

73

north of Germantown, where he turned down the Limekiln Road. Greene's mission was to envelop Howe's right and force the British back against the Schuylkill.

To the far left, Brigadier General David Forman and Brigadier General William Smallwood led their New Jersey and Maryland militia in an attempt to get behind the right rear of the British. The reserve was Stirling's division, which was to move to Chestnut Hill, where it was to be ready to support either Greene's or Sullivan's wing.

Washington thought he had allowed time for almost two hours' rest after the men reached their pre-attack positions. Then they would move out at 4:00 A.M., striking the British outposts silently, with bayonet only, at 5:00, still an hour before dawn. His schedule was overoptimistic, however. To make things worse, General Greene's guide had lost his way on the dark roads and Greene was almost an hour further behind schedule than Sullivan and Washington.

Sullivan's lead brigade, commanded by Brigadier General Thomas Conway, finally deployed for attack on the British Mount Airy outpost at 6:00 A.M., just as a misty dawn was breaking. They still expected to take the British by surprise, but they had unfortunately been sighted on the march almost three hours earlier, and the outpost was alerted. The British, however, thought that this was only a raid.

The Fog and the Fortress

The alert British outposts fired and withdrew slowly in good order, to where the British 2nd Light Infantry was waiting.

The light infantry battalion delivered a volley and then counter-attacked. The 40th Foot was brought up beside the light infantry to form a line of battle across the road.

The Americans had not expected such resistance, but they did not panic. Their superior numbers soon carried them into the northern outskirts of Germantown. It was now the turn of the British to be surprised, because of the weight of the attack. Howe himself went forward to rally the light infantry, shaming them for fleeing a few rebels. But when grapeshot from the American artillery knocked leaves and branches onto his shoulder, Howe was convinced that the Americans were in great force. He hastily withdrew to prepare for battle.

The morning mist now settled into a heavy fog that became an important part of the battle, confusing British and Americans alike. It was especially handicapping to Washington and his commanders, however, since they were on unfamiliar ground and had many separate forces to concentrate.

As Washington and Sullivan pushed into Germantown, they realized that there was no firing on their left, where Greene should have been making the main effort. Because of this, Sullivan shifted Wayne's brigade east of the main road, to protect his left flank. As a result, the weight of Sullivan's attack thus shifted somewhat eastward. Washington decided that he should now commit his reserve—Stirling's division—to make up for Greene's absence, and to further protect Sullivan's open left flank.

By this time the 40th Foot and the 2nd Light Infantry were falling back rapidly and in considerable disorder past the house of Judge Chew. This was a solid stone building just east of Germantown's main street and north of the center of town.

75

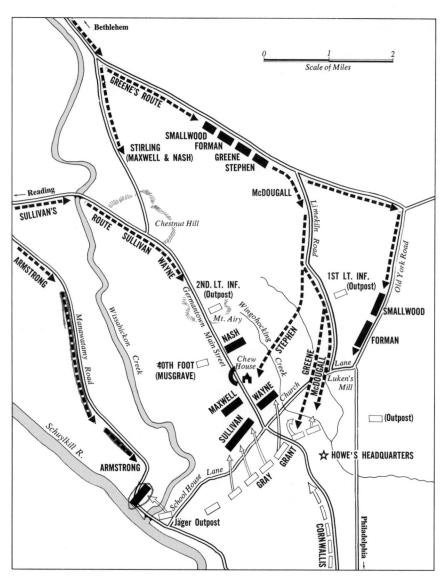

Battle of Germantown, October 4, 1777.

British Lieutenant Colonel Thomas Musgrave, commander of the 40th Foot, gathered about 120 of his fleeing men into the house and made it into a fortress, as the Americans streamed by on both sides of it. As Maxwell's brigade, from Stirling's reserve division, was deploying under Washington's supervision, musket fire blazed from the Chew House.

Washington was undecided whether to bypass the Chew House or delay his attack while it was reduced. He was persuaded, however, by his able artillery officer, General Knox, that the fortress must be taken. American artillery banged away at it, but most of the shot bounced off its sturdy stone walls. The fog prevented accurate aiming at the shuttered windows, in which Musgrave's men had made small holes for muskets.

After half an hour, Washington decided that the delay at the Chew House was too expensive. Both Stirling's reserve brigades were being held up far behind the main battle, when they were badly needed to support Sullivan, deeply involved in combat farther south. The Chew House could be taken care of later.

Victory to Defeat

Washington now learned that Greene had driven past the British outposts on the Limekiln Road, and was now engaged on the outskirts of the British camp, to the left of Wayne. From the sound of the firing, it seemed possible that Greene might actually be in the camp. Thinking that victory was almost won, Washington rode forward to rejoin Sullivan.

The battle was far from over, however. The firing to the left front increased in intensity, as British counterattacks halted

Battle of Germantown, October 4, 1777. Here is seen the fight around the Chew Mansion, the unexpected development that shattered Washington's plans and his hopes for victory. (Charles Phelps Cushing)

Greene's advance. Then came more firing from the left rear. The earlier firing at the Chew House had worried Wayne, who slowed his attack and sent some of his force back to investigate. Stephen, who should have been attacking on the left with Greene, had also been drawn far off course to the Chew House, where some of his men began a new effort to reduce the little fortress. The noise led some of Wayne's men to believe that they were being attacked from the rear, and they began to panic.

It was now about 9:00 A.M., and the British main army was fully engaged, having been given time to organize, thanks largely to the Chew House delays. British General Grant found the gap in the American line created by Stephen's prolonged detour to Chew House, and pushed through. Sullivan's and Wayne's men had wasted much ammunition in the early morning, firing through the fog at trees and fence posts. Now their cartridge boxes were empty. The panic in Wayne's brigade spread to adjacent units, and some of Greene's and Sullivan's troops also began to run.

At this time Cornwallis came up from Philadelphia with reinforcements. The pressure on Greene's division increased, and his flank was threatened by Grant's penetration. He was forced to order a withdrawal, but was able to save his guns. Reluctantly Washington stopped his efforts to halt the panic, and ordered Sullivan and Wayne to pull back to reorganize.

The two wide-circling attacks—Armstrong's on the right, and Smallwood's and Forman's on the left—also failed, because of delays and overcaution. Realizing that there was no chance of victory, Washington ordered a general withdrawal, and the Battle of Germantown was over.

The American defeat was the result of an overcomplicated

79

plan and bad luck. The confusion caused by the fog had also probably hurt them much more than it had affected the British, who were on the defensive on their own ground. The British had lost about 70 killed, 450 wounded, and 14 missing, while the American losses were 152 killed, 521 wounded, and almost 400 missing. Fortunately for American morale, Washington's men thought they had inflicted more casualties than they had suffered.

The battle in fact increased British respect for the Americans and for Washington. Howe was impressed by the fact that his opponent had fought so skillfully and effectively less than a month after the defeat at the Brandywine. He gave no thought to pursuing the Americans. Instead, he withdrew to Philadelphia and spent the next few weeks fortifying the city and opening his line of communications down the Delaware River, reducing several American forts on the riverbank.

CHAPTER 8

Monmouth Courthouse

Generals Are Changed and Exchanged

Early in 1778, General Sir Henry Clinton replaced General Howe as British commander in chief in North America. Along with his new command, Clinton received orders from London to evacuate Philadelphia, withdraw to New York, and go on the defensive. The American representatives in Paris had achieved spectacular success by signing a treaty of alliance with France. The British government had decided, in response, to concentrate its efforts in 1778 on operations in the southern colonies and on a naval campaign against France in the West Indies.

At about this same time, arrangements were made to exchange a captured British major general for American Major General Charles Lee, who had been a prisoner of war since December, 1776. Lee had been second in rank only to George Washington in 1775 and 1776, and had been a professional British soldier before the Revolution. In the early days of the war he had performed capably, and was honored by Washington and most of the American army as their outstanding professional officer.

Lee had begun to behave strangely, however, during the fall of 1776. Several times he had ignored or disobeyed orders from

Washington and during the dark days of November had stayed east of the Hudson after Washington had withdrawn to New Jersey. After he finally did come to New Jersey at Washington's insistence, Lee was captured by the British. As a prisoner, he had long talks on strategy with General Howe, and apparently gave him some advice on how to defeat the Americans, quite possibly committing treason in the process. But this was not known to the Americans. Washington warmly welcomed Lee when he was exchanged.

Clinton Prepares to Move

By late May of 1778 it was clear to Washington at Valley Forge that Clinton was preparing to leave Philadelphia. Shiploads of supplies and baggage went down the river every day. Washington heard rumors that the British were planning to go to New York and he prepared to take advantage of the evacuation. He decided to follow the British closely and harass them constantly, but not to attack unless an especially good opportunity presented itself.

Washington now had about 14,500 men, of whom nearly 12,000 were Continental troops. These men were well trained, thanks to the hard and imaginative work of the Prussian Baron von Steuben at Valley Forge during the winter. Washington knew that Clinton probably had about 16,000 men.

Another foreign volunteer, the young Marquis de Lafayette, was serving as a major general with the American forces at his own expense. Washington told Lafayette to be ready to pursue Clinton with an advance guard of six brigades, about 2,000 men in all, as soon as Philadelphia was evacuated. Anthony Wayne was Lafayette's second-in-command.

Pursuit Across New Jersey

It was 10:00 A.M. on June 18 when Washington learned that the British had crossed the Delaware that morning and were marching northeastward. Lafayette's brigades moved out immediately. A few hours later the remainder of the army followed.

The Americans made faster progress than the British in the intense summer heat, partly because they carried lighter packs. By June 23 Lafayette was south of Kingston, New Jersey. Washington and the main body of the army were at Hopewell, and both American groups were considerably closer to New York than Clinton, who had only reached the vicinity of Allentown.

By June 27, Clinton reached Monmouth Courthouse (now Freehold). Up to this time his route had been selected so as to give him the choice of going overland to New York or going to Sandy Hook, where he could then embark on ships to reach the city. The overland movement was simpler, but the area just west of the Hudson was cut by many streams, and Clinton realized that if he were forced to fight there he might be defeated in detail. Now, with Washington ahead of him on the land route, there could be only one choice, and Clinton determined to push east to Sandy Hook. First, however, he rested his hot and tired men all day at Monmouth Courthouse.

Up until this point, Clinton had marched his men on parallel roads so that they would not be widely dispersed and could be quickly deployed for battle. Washington guessed that Clinton would take the water route, and he knew that there was only one road running from Monmouth Courthouse toward Sandy Hook. He was determined to seize the opportunity for a decisive victory.

Lee and the Advance Guard

On June 26, Washington had more than doubled the strength of his advance guard to over 6,000 men in anticipation of striking Clinton's army quickly, as soon as it was stretched out on the single road. General Lee, as senior officer in the army after Washington, asked for the honor of commanding this force, and Washington approved, making Lafayette his second-in-command. Washington was a little reluctant to assign Lee to this important command, because up to this time Lee had opposed aggressive action, arguing that American troops could not stand up to British regulars. But it was traditional that the second most senior officer should be placed in command of an army's major detachment, and Washington could see no reason for denying Lee's request.

On June 27, while Clinton's army was resting, Washington ordered Lee to attack as soon as the British were on the road the next morning. The order was clear, and was accepted by Lee in the presence of several other American generals. Lee's force was at Englishtown, northwest of Monmouth, while Washington and the main army were farther west, between Englishtown and Cranbury.

Clinton, recognizing the danger of an American attack, had

84

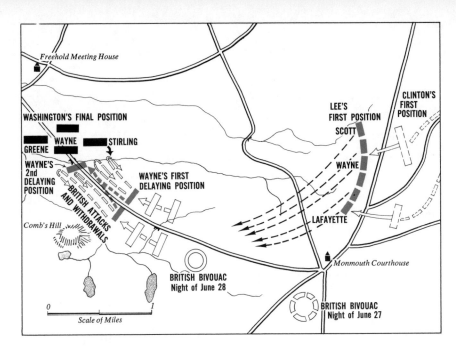

Battle of Monmouth.

divided his army into two portions. The leading division, about 6,000 strong, was under German General von Knyphausen, and would be followed by the army's supply train of 1,500 wagons. The main body of the army, probably slightly less than 10,000 men, would follow under General Cornwallis, with Clinton accompanying.

Knyphausen's leading contingent moved out at 4:00 A.M., June 28. An hour later Washington got the news. He immediately sent an order to Lee to attack. He promised Lee that he would bring up the main body of the American army to support him as soon as possible.

Despite Washington's orders of the day before, and this renewed and specific order to attack, Lee did nothing at all to

85

prepare for action, although he did start his troops on a slow march toward Monmouth Courthouse. His leading units arrived there somewhat after 10:00 A.M., as the last British were leaving. Lee issued no orders, but Lafayette and several brigade commanders attacked anyway. Clinton promptly turned Cornwallis around to deal with these piecemeal efforts. Still Lee gave no orders.

The Preliminary Encounter

It is not clear just what Lee did at that time. Although he issued no orders to his command, apparently he personally told one or two of his brigadiers to withdraw. As a result, some of the advanced guard units were still attacking while others were withdrawing, and the majority stood by useless, waiting for orders.

Clinton at once recognized that there was indecision among the Americans. He ordered Cornwallis to counterattack, and sent orders to Knyphausen to halt and send back 3,000 troops. In the face of Cornwallis' determined attack, most of the Americans broke and ran. Only Wayne's brigade, firing and falling back in good order, prevented disaster.

By this time it was about noon. Washington was passing Freehold Meeting House with the main body of the army. Disturbed by the sparse battle sounds, and puzzled that Lee and Lafayette did not seem to have engaged the enemy, the commander in chief was amazed to meet fleeing troops. He realized that the American advance guard must be retreating without

86

ever having joined battle. He at once galloped forward, accompanied by his staff. Soon he met Lee riding to the rear, apparently unconcerned about this turn of events.

"What, Sir, is the meaning of this? Whence come this disorder and confusion?" demanded Washington.

The scene has been described by several witnesses and depicted by artists, but no one can be sure now just what was said. Some witnesses later said that Washington, in an unusual burst of temper, cursed Lee; others denied this. All agree, however, that Washington clearly communicated his scorn and indignation to Lee. Then, wasting no more time, he rode forward to rally his men and salvage what he could of the situation. He soon met Wayne's hard-pressed brigade, still falling back in good order.

Washington Rallies the Army

Just 200 yards in front of the leading British, Washington gathered two more regiments to reinforce Wayne's delaying position. The general then rode back a few hundred yards, where he found a good battle position on a low ridge overlooking a shallow depression. He and his staff began rallying stragglers. As often in the past, Washington's commanding physical presence and determined personal leadership made the difference between success and rout.

Soon General Greene appeared, leading the main body of the army. Washington promptly put him in command of the right wing of the line he was building up. When Stirling's divi-

87

sion came up, Washington put him into position on Greene's left. Washington and Lafayette then began to create a reserve out of the fleeing remnants of Lee's command.

Wayne's infantry, supported by General Knox's artillery, was meanwhile delaying the British advance. But when Clinton brought up reinforcements and renewed the attack, Wayne had to withdraw. He pulled back to the edge of the depression, or ravine, taking a position between, and slightly in front of, Greene and Stirling.

The British now moved up opposite the American line, on the southern side of the shallow ravine, which was less than 100 yards wide. Clinton then ordered simultaneous attacks against the American center and the still-deploying left. Stirling, however, neatly brought his troops into line on the left and wheeled to envelop the right flank of the British infantry trying to cross the depression. The attackers fell back in confusion.

Clinton, meanwhile, was rapidly building up his own line. He made another massive assault against Wayne's brigade. But those troops, after firing a volley that slowed the British advance, fell back about 50 yards in good order. Wayne placed himself in the center of the American line, knowing that Stirling and Greene were now fully deployed.

The British rushed after Wayne, only to run into a steady fire from the entire American lines, and then an unexpected counterattack from Wayne's force. Astonished at the cool, professional fighting of the Americans, the leading British elements withdrew from the valley, and back out of range.

It was now after 5:00 P.M. Clinton broke off the infantry battle, but the artillery continued firing. It was at this time that the legendary Molly Pitcher (Mary Hays), after bringing water

88

Battle of Monmouth, June 28, 1778. This scene is probably intended to show Wayne's counterattack across the shallow ravine, the climactic event of the battle. (Charles Phelps Cushing)

to the thirsty American gunners, took her wounded husband's place at his cannon.

Finally the exhausted men of both sides stopped firing, and the Battle of Monmouth was over. The Americans reported that they had suffered 360 casualties, killed, wounded, and missing, of whom 40 were deaths from sunstroke in the 100-degree heat. The British reported 358 casualties, including 59 deaths from sunstroke. Actual losses on both sides were probably twice as high as reported.

At midnight the British broke camp and were safely away before the Americans awoke. They reached Sandy Hook, and made good their escape to New York. For Washington the battle was heartening in its demonstration of the value of the Valley Forge training program. But the failure to gain a decisive victory because of Lee's inexplicable behavior was a bitter disappointment.

As for Lee, he offered no explanation. In fact he had the effrontery to demand either a court-martial or an apology from Washington because of the public tongue-lashing the commander in chief had given him near Freehold Meeting House. He received the court-martial, and suspension from his command. He was eventually dismissed from the army by Congress.

CHAPTER 9

Stony Point

Clinton Strikes North

Two years after Washington's disastrous campaign around New York City in 1776, he was back near Manhattan Island. This time, however, it was the British who were defending the island, and the Americans who were the besiegers.

Washington disposed his forces in a wide arc around the blockaded city. The American positions ringed New York with a land blockade and also protected the vital communications line between New England and the states to the south. Washington now had 16,800 men, his largest army up to that time, and many of them had been well trained at Valley Forge and were battle hardened.

Numerous raids by both sides and skirmishes between patrols took place in 1778 and early 1779. Then in May, 1779, Clinton decided to capture two American forts on the Hudson, as a check on any contemplated American advance southward, and as bases for possible future operations of his own. On May 30 he led a picked force of 6,000 men up the river, and on June 1 they landed at the south end of the area called the Hudson Highlands, where the river flows in zigzag curves through elevated terrain. His objectives were Stony Point on the west bank and Verplanck's Point on the east bank. Some earthwork fortifications had been begun on Stony Point, but the British took the little post without opposition. Fort Lafayette on Verplanck's Point put up stiff resistance, but its little 70-man garrison was soon overwhelmed.

Possession of these two forts gave the British control of both ends of King's Ferry, where the main north-south highway crossed the Hudson. Clinton moved swiftly to make Stony Point a virtually impregnable fortress.

The Defenses of Stony Point

Stony Point projects like an arrowhead out into the river, and is surrounded by water on three sides. It rises 150 feet above the river and has steep sides of bare rock. On this promontory Clinton had a citadel built, surrounded by artillery batteries that were connected by trenches. To protect the land approaches to the fort, two successive arcs of abatis were constructed. These were made of sharpened tree trunks, pointed out toward any approaching enemy, interlaced with timbers and firmly secured. At high tide the fortified area was an island that could be reached only by a causeway across the surrounding marsh. Clinton left about 700 men at Stony Point, under the command of Lieutenant Colonel Henry Johnson. He also left a smaller garrison at Fort Lafayette, and the sloop HMS *Vulture* was at anchor in the river to provide gun support to both forts.

One of Washington's most able and experienced commanders, Brigadier General Anthony Wayne, proposed to capture the seemingly invulnerable Stony Point fort with an apparent brash-

92

ness that amazed the other American commanders. Although Washington approved Wayne's plan, other American officers began to call him "Mad Anthony."

Wayne's Plan

Two years earlier, at Paoli, Pennsylvania, Wayne's brigade had been the victims of a surprise, silent, nighttime bayonet British assault. Wayne had gotten most of his men away safely, but he had not forgotten the horror or the effectiveness of the "Paoli Massacre." He decided to make use of the lesson, and turn it against his teachers.

Wayne and his hand-picked, well-trained brigade of 1,300 set out on the morning of July 15, 1779. They marched 13 miles to their jump-off point, about a mile from Stony Point, and then Wayne gave them their orders.

Each man was ordered on pain of death to keep his unloaded musket on his shoulder throughout the march and up to the moment of attack. No word was to be spoken. The men would approach the fort in two columns, with Wayne leading one group through the swamp to strike from the right and Colonel Richard Butler leading the other group farther north along the causeway to strike from the left. Ahead of each column moved 150 men with axes, assigned to chop a way through the abatis, followed by 20 men and an officer, volunteers who were to rush immediately through the openings and attack with the bayonet. Cash awards were promised to the first men inside the fort.

The final feature of the carefully prepared plan was a much

93

smaller third force, advancing between the other two, whose men had loaded muskets and were ordered to fire on the fort as soon as the assault began, creating a diversion.

"The Fort's Our Own"

It was impossible to move through the mud and water of the swamp in complete silence, but by the time the British pickets detected the attackers the axes were almost ready to go into action. Gaps began to appear in the outer abatis, and then the inner; the eager troops worked their way in, undeterred by British musket fire. At this point a blaze of American musket fire broke out in the center as the little demonstration force carried out its mission.

British Colonel Johnson responded as Wayne had hoped, rushing half his garrison down to the abatis in the area of the American fire, while on both sides of him the silent bayonet forces moved through the first abatis, then the second, and then over the parapet and into the citadel itself. A French volunteer, Lieutenant Colonel François de Fleury, won the $500 award as the first man in.

Once within the outer abatis the silent Americans began shouting incessantly and at the tops of their voices, "The fort's our own!" This final touch of Wayne's, part of the men's original orders, was an effective bit of psychological warfare. Confused and panic-stricken British began surrendering wholesale, and by the time Colonel Johnson realized what was happening, it was too late to get his center force into action. The whole battle was over in thirty minutes, with 63 British dead, more than 70

94

Storming of Stony Point, July 16, 1779. Wayne leads his column across the abatis, just behind the storming party. About this time Wayne was slightly wounded, and momentarily stunned by a glancing blow of a musket ball against his head. Scrambling to his feet, and propped up by two of his men, he insisted upon continuing at the head of the assaulting column. (Charles Phelps Cushing)

wounded, 543 captured, and the fort in American hands. The captors promptly turned the Stony Point guns on the British sloop *Vulture*, and the ship quickly moved downstream.

The American losses had been surprisingly light—15 killed and 80 wounded—considering the dangerous mission of the

95

leading troops. The victory was greeted by the American army and public with incredulous joy. Congress awarded Wayne a gold medal, and gave each man in his command a share of the cash value of the supplies captured.

Despite the victory, Wayne continued to be known as "Mad Anthony." Boldness and imagination he certainly had, but "mad" was an ironic nickname for an officer whose striking success came, above all, from careful planning and the firm leadership of thoroughly trained and disciplined troops.

CHAPTER 10

Camden

Clinton Moves South

After three years of vain attempts to destroy Washington's army, and to split New England from the other states farther south, Britain found herself faced with an alliance between the rebel government and powerful France. As a result the British government changed strategy in early 1778. General Clinton was ordered to start a campaign to reconquer the southern states. The high command in London had decided it would be best to work up from the south, where there were many Loyalists, rather than attack the rebel strongholds in New England and the central states directly. A sea offensive against the French navy in the West Indies was also in the plans.

In accordance with his instructions, Clinton sent forces to Georgia and South Carolina in 1778, but at first the new southern strategy did not go well for the British. By late 1779 the port of Savannah was under siege by a French naval force and an American army under Major General Benjamin Lincoln. Clinton decided, therefore, to take matters firmly into his own hands. On December 26, 1779, he and General Cornwallis sailed southward from New York with 8,500 picked troops.

The siege of Savannah had been lifted by the time Clinton

arrived at the Georgia coast, so he immediately moved north after Lincoln, who had retreated into South Carolina. Through a combined land and sea offensive, Clinton cornered Lincoln and his army in Charleston. After a long siege, Lincoln surrendered to Clinton on May 12, 1780.

De Kalb and Gates

Up in New York, meanwhile, Washington had dispatched additional reinforcements in the hope of saving Charleston. In command was a German soldier of fortune, who was a veteran of the French army: Major General Baron Johann de Kalb, a huge man physically and proven a brave and intelligent commander. De Kalb's division of Maryland and Delaware Continentals was small but excellent. One of its two brigades, under Brigadier General Mordecai Gist, was probably made up of the best men in the American army. In all, de Kalb had about 1,300 men.

De Kalb was in southern Virginia when he learned that Charleston had fallen, and he was uncertain of what to do next. He continued to move south, but had trouble feeding his troops, since the North Carolina civil authorities would give him no supplies. By early July he had reached Ramsey's Mill on the Deep River, where he was joined by Colonel Charles Armand and the remnants—about 120 men—of the Pulaski Legion. This was a force of British deserters and foreign officers whose original Polish commander had been killed at Savannah. Resting at the Deep River, de Kalb decided to move on to Camden, South Carolina, by a somewhat roundabout route that would take him through Patriot territory that was also good farmland.

At this point, de Kalb received news that a new commander for the Southern Department, replacing the captured Lincoln, was on his way south. De Kalb stayed at Ramsey's Mill, awaiting the arrival of Major General Horatio Gates.

Gates had been in command at Saratoga, and though he had little to do with the victory, had claimed all of the credit. He had long cultivated the favor of Congress, and Congress had given him this new appointment, despite Washington's strong preference for Nathanael Greene. Gates arrived on July 25 and promptly overrode de Kalb's recommendations on the route to Camden. After gathering some local militiamen, Gates took the direct road south, which went through a swampy, sandy region where there was little food and few people. Most of the scattered population were Tories and provided little help.

Gates crossed the Pee Dee River and arrived at Lynch's Creek on August 11, to find Colonel Lord Francis Rawdon with 1,000 British troops facing him from high ground across the creek. De Kalb urged a night march up the creek by his own division that would envelop Rawdon's left, cutting him off from Camden. As during the Saratoga campaign, Gates hesitated, and Rawdon fell back to join Cornwallis at Camden.

Then Gates made another mistake. He sent 100 Maryland Continentals and 300 North Carolina militia to help the partisan fighter Colonel Thomas Sumter attack a British supply train. Since Gates knew that Cornwallis was joining Rawdon with reinforcements, it is hard to understand why he weakened his force rather than attacking Rawdon immediately with all of his strength. He could have called on Sumter to join in such an attack, instead of striking the supply train.

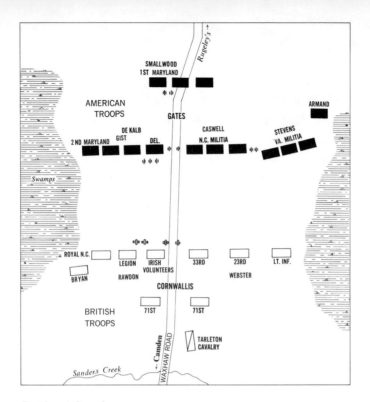

Battle of Camden.

Suddenly, on August 15, Gates decided to move. He ordered his 3,052 effective troops to make a night march to Camden. Almost 2,000 of these men were recently joined militia, and de Kalb protested that they were not well enough trained for a night march. Armand also protested that his legion, made up of cavalry and mounted infantry, should not lead the march as Gates ordered. He pointed out that it was almost impossible for horsemen to approach an objective in silence.

Gates brushed aside these protests. Soon after dark the men moved out from their base at Rugeley's Mill, after a half-cooked meal and a ration of molasses, specifically ordered by Gates as a substitute for unavailable rum. Already weakened by dysen-

100

tery, and further tormented by the impact of this food on their digestive tracts, most of the men were exhausted by the time they went into battle.

Meanwhile, Cornwallis and his 2,300 men had also set out on a night march, intending to catch the Americans by surprise at Rugeley's Mill. At 2:00 A.M. the vans of the two forces clashed in an unexpected encounter. Tarleton's Legion of American Tories charged Armand's Legion. Armand's outnumbered men fell back, but the Continental troops behind them held firm, and the fighting died away.

Disaster and Heroism

Gates's intended surprise attack was now an impossibility, and de Kalb urged withdrawal. Gates decided, however, on the advice of Brigadier General Edward Stevens, that it was too late to retreat, and the American force prepared for a morning battle.

The battlefield was an area of firm ground in a fairly open pinewoods, with the road on which the armies had been traveling running down the center. Both flanks of both armies were protected by swamps. Little Sanders Creek ran behind the British lines. The Americans were on slightly higher ground than their opponents.

Gates deployed his troops with General Stevens' 700 Virginia militia on the left, the 1,200 North Carolina militia in the center, and General Gist's brigade of crack Continentals from Maryland and Delaware on the right. Armand's Legion was just to the left and rear of the Virginia militia, and Brigadier Gen-

101

eral William Smallwood's 1st Maryland Brigade, probably fewer than 500 men, was drawn up behind the center. Gates placed himself in the center, behind the North Carolinians and in front of Smallwood, with his capable adjutant general, Colonel Otho Williams, at his side. De Kalb commanded the right wing.

The British marched to the attack in parallel columns, and began to deploy when they were about 200 yards from the Americans. Cornwallis put 1,000 British regulars under Lieutenant Colonel James Webster on the right, and some 800 Tory infantry on the left under Rawdon. Two battalions of regulars—about 400 men—were kept in reserve, along with 150 of Tarleton's cavalry.

As the British began to deploy for battle, Colonel Williams urged Gates to have the Virginia militia attack the British light infantry, on the British right flank, before they were ready for battle. Gates agreed, and Williams rushed forward with the message, but the tired and frightened Virginians would not attack on Stevens' order, nor could Williams get them to move.

The British completed their deployment, and Webster's regulars promptly advanced with bayonets fixed. They halted, fired a volley, then charged. The Virginians broke and ran, and the North Carolina militia beside them crumbled too. Armand's little force, isolated on the far left, also fell back, and of the first line only de Kalb and the Continentals were left.

Gates seems to have tried briefly to rally the militia, but very early in the battle he disappeared from the field. He arrived in Charlotte, North Carolina, 60 miles away, the same night. This feat of horsemanship ended his military career.

Back on the battlefield, no one could find General Small-

102

Battle of Camden, August 16, 1780. The last Americans on the field are overwhelmed by the victorious British. General De Kalb, about to be wounded for the eleventh time, is seen lying in the center of the picture. (Charles Phelps Cushing)

wood, whose 1st Maryland Brigade was the only force that could restore the American line. Leadership fell to Williams and de Kalb. Williams took command of Smallwood's brigade and brought it forward in an effort to replace the scattered militia on de Kalb's left. But the British had already reached that position, and they managed to drive a wedge between de Kalb and Williams. The British reserves now came into action, with Tarleton's cavalry striking the American center and hammering at the right of the Maryland brigade. Heavily outnumbered and under attack from two directions, the Marylanders finally broke and fled.

De Kalb and Gist were now alone on the field, the fine soldiers of their surrounded brigade outnumbered four to one. They had already fought off several attacks, and now de Kalb reorganized them to fight in two directions. To the astonishment of the British he ordered a bayonet charge. Probably the most intense hand-to-hand fighting of the entire war took place in the next few minutes. De Kalb himself finally fell, wounded eleven times, as Tarleton's cavalry made a final charge, and the surrounded survivors surrendered. De Kalb died in the British camp a few hours later, one of the great military heroes of the Revolution.

The Americans lost about 600 men killed in the Battle of Camden and about 1,000 captured, many of whom were wounded. The British officially reported 79 killed and 245 wounded, but the true figures must have been considerably higher. In any case, Cornwallis was well on his way to Virginia —and Yorktown.

CHAPTER 11

Cowpens

New Command Team in the South

After the disaster at Camden, Congress asked Washington to appoint a successor to Gates in command of the Southern Department. The commander in chief at once ordered General Nathanael Greene to take this post.

Meanwhile, as soon as he heard the report of the defeat, Colonel Daniel Morgan, who had been in retirement in Virginia, had ridden to Gates's new headquarters, at Charlotte, North Carolina, to offer his services.

No ordinary man could have done what Morgan did. He had never fully recovered from the ill effects of a winter in Canada as a prisoner of war after he had been captured at Quebec on New Year's day, 1776. Despite painful and crippling arthritis, he had become one of Washington's most trusted and reliable subordinates as the leader of a rifle brigade, and had performed heroically in the two battles of Saratoga, where he earned the bitter enmity of Horatio Gates. When, as a result of Gates's influence, and despite Washington's recommendation, Congress had refused to promote him to brigadier general, Morgan had retired in disgust to his farm in Virginia. Now, in a time of grave crisis, ignoring his physical disabilities, he forgot his hatred and contempt for Gates and volunteered to serve under his old enemy.

Undoubtedly Morgan was greatly relieved when Gates was removed from command and replaced by Greene. And he was also heartened to learn that Congress had belatedly accepted Washington's recommendation and promoted him to brigadier general. Wholeheartedly he threw himself into his duties as the junior member of the new command team taking over in the southern theater of war.

Greene Divides His Forces

Greene's first important command decision was almost a catastrophe. Although his total force was much smaller than that of British General Cornwallis, Greene divided it in two, sending Morgan southwest into western South Carolina with about 600 men. There Morgan was to act as a rallying point for local militia and to threaten a British fortified post called Ninety-Six. Greene himself took 1,000 men southeast to Cheraw, South Carolina. He seems to have hoped that his little army could forage for supplies more easily if it was less concentrated and that two forces could threaten more British posts than one could. Apparently he did not think of the fact that the British could also concentrate overwhelming force against either detachment. In any case, Greene moved out on December 19 and Morgan the next day. By Christmas Day the two generals were 140 miles apart.

Morgan's force, camped near the Pacolet River, had grown to about 1,000 by attracting several militia units. On December 28 Morgan sent out a raiding party under Colonel William

Washington, who made a successful lightning attack on a body of Tory raiders near Ninety-Six.

Pricked to action, Cornwallis sent Colonel Banastre Tarleton with one-third the British force, about 1,120 men, to deal with Morgan. As Tarleton understood his mission, it was to "destroy Morgan's corps or push it before me over the Broad River toward Kings Mountain."* Cornwallis himself planned to move the main body of his army north between Greene and Morgan as soon as he received 1,500 expected reinforcements under Major General Alexander Leslie.

Tarleton Approaches

Tarleton moved out on New Year's Day of 1781. He led a formidable force, not significantly larger than Morgan's, but made up entirely of fine fighting units. First there was his own British Legion, a crack unit of American Tories, 200 dragoons and 200 mounted infantry. The sight of their green coats inspired fear and anger among American troops and in Patriot communities throughout the south. Tarleton also had a 300-man battalion of the 7th Foot and another of the 71st Highlanders—both excellent regular infantry—plus 100 men of the 17th Light Dragoons, and a small artillery force with two 3-pounder guns.

* King's Mountain, by coincidence, had been the site of an American victory on October 7. A 1,200-man, all-militia force—mostly North Carolinians—had stormed up its wooded slopes and captured or killed every man of a Tory force of 1,000. King's Mountain showed what Patriot militiamen could do, balancing some of the less creditable actions of other militia units.

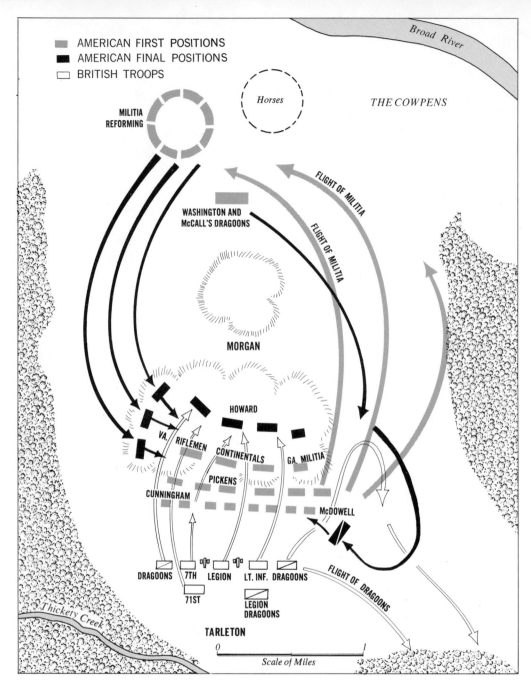

Battle of the Cowpens.

On January 15, Morgan learned through excellent cavalry reconnaissance that Tarleton was approaching and what his strength was. Next day, when he learned that Tarleton was crossing the Pacolet River, Morgan moved back 8 miles, across a more northerly tributary of the Broad River called Thicketty Creek. He camped that night in the bend of the Broad River, with the creek in front of him. The area was called the Cowpens because the farmers of the area gathered their cattle in the bend there before sending them off to market. Again intelligence reports from Colonel Washington told Morgan where Tarleton was—encamped at the spot near the Pacolet that Morgan had just left.

Plan of Battle

Morgan deployed his men where the Broad River was separated from Thicketty Creek by about 5 miles of cleared land. In the center of the field was a gently rising hill that commanded the surrounding wooded areas and thus secure against surprise envelopments. For further protection, Morgan placed a line of pickets on the far side of Thicketty Creek and sent out more mounted patrols.

Morgan's strength was now about 1,100, but more than half of it was militia. His chief problem, as he saw it, was how to get the most good and least harm from these unreliable troops. They had signed up to fight the enemy, and they knew how to shoot, but they were not trained for pitched battle against regular army units. They were not used to military discipline, and they did not want to be killed. Over and over, fleeing

109

militia had brought about American defeats in this war, most recently in the disaster near Camden, still fresh in Morgan's mind.

Morgan drew up his troops in three lines. His 300 reliable Maryland and Delaware Continentals, under Lieutenant Colonel John E. Howard, were placed farthest back, just forward of the crest of the hill. On their right were nearly 200 veteran Virginia rifle militiamen, and on their left some of the better Georgia militia. Howard was in command of this line. The second line was about 200 yards ahead, on the slope of the hill. Here were about 300 militia from North and South Carolina under the command of Colonel Andrew Pickens, a successful partisan leader. About a third of these militiamen were Pickens' own guerrilla veterans. The line farthest forward was made up of about 150 Georgia and North Carolina militiamen. They were all riflemen and good shots, but Morgan felt sure they could not stand firm against a charge by British regulars. Their commanders were Major John Cunningham of Georgia and Major Charles McDowell of North Carolina.

Morgan also had a mounted reserve, under Colonel Washington's command, placed behind a second hill. It included 30 to 40 South Carolina militia horsemen under Lieutenant Colonel James McCall and perhaps 20 more mounted militiamen from other units, as well as Washington's 80 Continental dragoons. Morgan gave the mounted militiamen sabers, thus converting them to cavalry. Near them were gathered the horses of all the other militiamen, and Morgan made sure that everyone knew where the horses were.

The sharpshooters in the first line and the men in Pickens' second line were not expected to hold long, and Morgan did not

110

order them to. With a masterful understanding of psychology, he gave them instead a task he thought they were equal to— "Just hold up your heads, boys, three fires and you're free." If they waited until the enemy was 50 yards away and then fired three volleys, they could withdraw, and Morgan made it clear that in his eyes this would be praiseworthy soldiering and a great deed for the Patriot cause.

Again and again Morgan repeated his refrain over the campfires that night. Morale was high in the American camp when Morgan himself roused the men in the predawn blackness with the news that Tarleton's troops were coming.

"Old Morgan Was Never Beaten!"

The militia sharpshooters fired first as Tarleton's dragoons rode forward to probe the American positions. The dragoons, surprised by the accurate fire of the Americans, withdrew. Tarleton then sent his entire command forward in battle deployment. The infantry of his own British Legion formed the center, with the elite light infantry companies of the 7th Foot and 71st Highlanders on the right and the rest of the 7th Foot on the left. One gun was placed immediately to each side of the Legion infantry. The 17th Light Dragoons were on the flanks of the infantry line, and the Legion dragoons and the main body of the 71st Highlanders were in reserve.

As the awesome mass of brightly uniformed British and Tories marched forward, Morgan's chief concern was to keep the men from shooting too soon, with the British still beyond effective range. He seems to have used the same words attributed

111

to General Putnam at the Battle of Bunker's Hill: "Don't fire until you see the whites of their eyes."

As the British approached they gave a chilling war cry. The Americans answered with another, and then fired the first of the volleys Morgan had ordered. Gaps opened in the British lines, as the rifles took a heavy toll, and then were quickly closed by the disciplined regulars. A second American volley rang out. Some of the first-line marksmen may have stayed to fire a third, but most of them apparently now fell back to Pickens' line or fled toward their horses. The British infantry-men were advancing quickly with bayonets gleaming. Pickens' men thinned their ranks further, but also broke and ran after firing one or two volleys. The British dragoons rode forward to cut down the militia as they ran, but at this point Colonel Washington and his cavalry command rode up from behind the hill, driving off the surprised British horsemen.

Meanwhile, the fleeing militiamen, dashing for their horses, found the way blocked by Morgan, who urged them to regroup. "Form, form, my brave fellows!" he shouted. "Give them one more fire and the day is ours. Old Morgan was never beaten." Form they did, probably further encouraged to stay by the sight of the unfordable river beyond them. Leaving Pickens to reorganize them, Morgan dashed forward to rejoin Howard and his Continentals.

While Morgan had been rallying the militiamen, the steady fire of the Continentals in the third line had halted the British advance. Tarleton decided to take the 71st Highlanders out of reserve and send them around Colonel Howard's right flank. Responding, Howard ordered his right to wheel right to face this threat. The order was misunderstood, however, and the right wing began withdrawing, leaving the rest of the American main line exposed. Howard quickly ordered a general withdrawal, to the horror of Morgan, who now came on the scene to find his best troops marching to the rear. Howard explained the situation, and the relieved general went back to find a place to form a new line.

Like Morgan, Tarleton interpreted Howard's withdrawal as a retreat. He thought the battle was won, and ordered his men to charge. At this moment, Morgan received a message from Colonel Washington, who had reformed his cavalry and was ready to charge the British right. At the same time the Carolina and Georgia militiamen reappeared in fighting order under Pickens' command, ready to strike the British left.

With Washington's horsemen and Pickens' militia ready to attack, Morgan ordered the Continentals to halt and fire on the advancing British. Obediently they turned, released a volley, and then, on order, charged forward with fixed bayonets. Tarleton's leading men were totally amazed by this unexpected counterattack. They turned and ran, as the Continentals bore down on them. At this moment Washington's horsemen charged with flashing sabers against the British from the right rear, and the resurrected militiamen drove in from the left.

Tarleton was back with his Legion dragoons, who had not yet been committed. He ordered them to charge, but they refused. He charged himself, with a few obedient followers, then saw that the battle was hopelessly lost. He turned and fled. During the ensuing pursuit by Washington's cavalry, there was a dramatic personal saber duel between Washington and Tarleton. Then Tarleton turned and galloped off with the pitiful remnant of his little army.

113

Battle of the Cowpens, January 17, 1781. Tarleton's horsemen are seen fleeing from the battlefield; this is probably intended to depict a brief inconclusive, personal encounter between Colonel Tarleton and Colonel Washington. (Charles Phelps Cushing)

Morgan's men had killed 110 British and captured more than 800. They had also taken the two British guns and large numbers of muskets and horses. The Americans had lost only 12 killed and 61 wounded. Morgan had won a victory unparalleled in tactical perfection during the Revolution, with a morale-building power much like that of General Washington's victories at Trenton and Princeton.

Morgan was fortunate that his subordinates, Howard, Pickens, and Washington, were men worthy of their commander. His leadership was decisive, however, and he demonstrated its quality again in his actions immediately after the battle. Without even pausing to count or bury his dead he quit the battlefield within an hour. Knowing well that Cornwallis would be hot on his trail, he rushed his men northeast toward the crossing of the Little Catawba River. He knew that unless he could rejoin Greene before Cornwallis thrust his much larger force between them, the victory at Cowpens would turn to dust and ashes.

CHAPTER 12

Guilford Courthouse

Pursuit and Maneuver

Daniel Morgan's victory at Cowpens was his last battle. His arthritis became unbearable in the chill dampness of the Carolina winter. What little sleep he got during the exhausting month-long retreat that followed was in wet clothes, on the cold ground, wrapped in a soggy blanket. Greene, learning that the brave Virginian was near his physical breaking point, left his own command in the hands of Brigadier General Isaac Huger and joined Morgan early in the retreat. By February 6, when the two segments of the American Southern Army rejoined at Guilford Courthouse, Morgan could no longer sit his horse. Greene sent him back to his Virginia home.

Greene now had 1,400 Continental troops and 600 much less reliable militiamen. He briefly considered standing and fighting, but decided that he had no hope of victory against Cornwallis' army of almost 3,000 regular troops. Greene moved out toward the lower Dan River, where he had already ordered all available boats to be gathered in case of need. After a dramatic pursuit, Cornwallis arrived at the south bank of the river just in time to see the last Americans crossing, and all the boats for miles around gone with them.

116

Cornwallis, having failed in his effort to catch the retreating Americans, withdrew to Hillsboro for rest and supplies. He detached some units to protect his line of communications back to Camden and Charleston. Then he began a series of maneuvers in an attempt to lure Greene into battle.

Cautiously Greene returned southward. When he again arrived at Guilford Courthouse on March 14, he decided the time for battle had come. He now had 4,300 men, of whom 1,600 were Continental infantry and 160 were Continental cavalry. Cornwallis probably had fewer than 2,000 troops, but all first-class regulars.

Greene's Dispositions

Greene selected a favorable defensive position just south of Guilford Courthouse, and astride the main north-south road through central North Carolina. The courthouse was located near the top of a commanding ridge, and Greene emplaced his troops in a thinly wooded area on the southern slopes. He adopted a plan very similar to the one Morgan had used at the Cowpens. There were to be three battle lines, with the least reliable troops in the front line, and the most reliable in the third and main line of defense.

The first line was at the base of the courthouse ridge, where the ground began to rise from a shallow valley. This line was made up of the North Carolina militia. They were stationed at the edge of a woods behind a picket fence that overlooked a large clearing to the south. To their right, sheltered by woods, were 200 Virginia riflemen under Colonel Charles Lynch, and still farther right was Captain Robert Kirkwood's Delaware light infantry, an elite Continental outfit. Colonel William Washington and his 80 mounted troops were on the extreme right, protecting the flank. The left side of the line was organized in the same way, with its riflemen under Colonel Richard Campbell and with the flank protected by the light infantry and cavalry of Colonel Henry ("Light-Horse Harry") Lee's Legion. Greene was following Morgan's written advice in placing the rifle marksmen on the flanks, where they could direct enfilade fire against the flanks of the advancing enemy.

Three hundred yards farther back was the second line, made up of Virginia militia. One brigade was to the west of the main road under Brigadier General Edward Stevens; the other was to the east under Brigadier General Robert Lawson.

Because of the nature of the ground, the third line was not directly behind the first two, but was 500 yards behind the right wing of the second line, entirely to the west of the main north-south road that bisected the battlefield. Here there was a sharply rising slope with a commanding view of the main road and the surrounding lightly wooded countryside. Behind this main line was the courthouse itself, at the northwest corner of the junction where the main road met one coming in from the west. The troops in this final line were the Continentals—General Huger commanding the 4th and 5th Virginia Regiments on the right and Colonel Otho Williams commanding the 1st and 5th Maryland Regiments on the left.

Greene's three lines were considerably farther apart than Morgan's had been at Cowpens. The men of the second line could barely see the front line through the trees. Coordinated

118

action would therefore be difficult. Greene himself planned to take position behind the third line, at the courthouse.

While waiting for the British to arrive, Greene spent most of his time with the militia. He followed Morgan's psychological approach. Since he felt sure the militia would break and run sooner or later, he tried to make it later by giving them a definite and limited task to perform. "Three rounds, my boys, and then you may fall back," he told them again and again, using Morgan's battle-proven formula.

Cornwallis Moves to Battle

When Cornwallis learned of Greene's approach, late on the fourteenth, his small army was about 12 miles south of Guilford Courthouse. He got his troops on the march early the following morning. Since food was short, and since he wanted to engage Greene before the Americans could change their mind about fighting, he had his men march without breakfast. So, about five hours later, at the end of a 12-mile march, and a brief skirmish with Lee's men, spread out in front of the American position as a delaying force, the British troops were hungry.

As Lee's Legion moved back, to take up position on the left of the first American line, the British moved up until they reached the southern edge of the clearing in front of the North Carolina militia. Two American cannon, stationed in the road, in the center of the line, immediately opened fire.

Two British artillery pieces were quickly unlimbered to reply to this fire, while Cornwallis deployed his troops. He placed

Major General Alexander Leslie's brigade on the right, with Colonel von Bose's Hessian regiment farthest right, a battalion of the 71st Highlanders left of it, and the 1st Battalion of the Guards centered behind them. Left of the main road that bisected the battlefield was the brigade of Lieutenant Colonel James Webster, including the 23rd Foot (Royal Welsh Fusiliers) next to the road, the 33rd Regiment to the far left, and placed behind them, a company of Hessian jaegers (light infantry riflemen) and the light infantry companies of the rest of the army. Lieutenant Colonel Charles O'Hara was in command of a small reserve contingent that included the Guards 2nd Battalion and all the grenadier companies.

The First Line

As the British and Hessian troops advanced into the clearing, about 1:30 P.M., the North Carolina militiamen fired their first volley, and a second. Gaps appeared in the advancing lines. The British halted briefly to fire a return volley, then Webster ordered his men to charge. When the flashing British bayonets approached, the North Carolina militia ran.

As the British surged forward into the wooded area beyond the fence where the American first line had been, they still saw their comrades falling, and realized that accurate American fire was coming from their flanks. It was from the Virginia riflemen Greene had placed in the woods to the right and left of his first line. Leslie's and Webster's flank battalions wheeled to face the flanking fire. The Virginia riflemen, Kirkwood's light infantry, and Washington's horsemen on the American right flank fell

120

back in good order before Webster's men, taking prearranged positions on the right flank of the American second line. The American riflemen and Lee's troops on the left flank, however, were pushed to the northeast and isolated from the rest of the American force. Leslie left his Hessian troops to deal with this pocket and led the rest of his force forward against the left wing of the American second line.

The Second and Third Lines

Most of the Virginia militiamen of the second line held their ground, as the British approached. But on the far left Webster urged his men forward and slowly began to push back the American right flank, repulsing a counterattack by Washington's horsemen and Kirkwood's light infantry. Soon the right flank of Stevens' brigade was forced back, the brigade pivoting on the center of the line like a swinging door until it was at right angles to its original front. Then it was pushed east of the road, and finally it crumbled. The Virginians fled. On the British right, however, Leslie was still held up by Lawson's brigade.

While Leslie dealt with the remaining Virginians, Webster advanced toward the third American line, the solid Continentals on the hillside. As the British stormed up the hill, they met heavy fire from the waiting Continentals. As the British and Hessians hesitated, they were struck by a bayonet counterattack of the Virginia Continentals and driven back to the left rear, across a ravine, away from the main body of the British force.

Greene's battle plan had worked well. Despite the expected

121

flight of the North Carolina militia, an American victory was ready to be plucked. The British right had been stopped and the left was now thrown back. An all-out counterattack would surely have carried the day. Greene was too cautious to risk it, however, and the opportunity passed.

Lawson's brigade of Virginians finally gave way under Leslie's repeated assaults, with support from O'Hara's reserve, which moved into the center of the line. The British right wing now swept forward to envelop the left of the American third line, while Webster re-formed his men and moved back against the American right. As Colonel Williams shifted his Maryland brigade to meet the threatened envelopment of his left flank, the 5th Maryland Continentals became disorganized. This was a new unit that was not yet steady enough to meet the terror of a well-coordinated British musket volley followed by a bayonet charge. The Marylanders ran.

In the earlier fighting Colonel O'Hara had been wounded, but Lieutenant Colonel Duncan Stuart took his place in command of the center of the British line. Seeing the gap created in the American line as the 5th Maryland fled, Stuart led a charge toward the courthouse. But just as the American line seemed to be cut in two, Colonel Washington's little cavalry force counterattacked. Stuart was killed and the wounded O'Hara resumed command as the British center withdrew in confusion.

Battle in the Balance

Then the 1st Maryland Regiment, now under the able veteran Colonel John E. Howard of Cowpens fame, counterattacked

122

O'Hara's shattered regiments, which were saved only by the arrival of Leslie's units. A fire fight between Leslie's brigade and Howard's Marylanders raged around the courthouse. Again the tide of battle swung in favor of the Americans, as the Virginia Continentals began to drive Webster's brigade back down the hill.

At this point Cornwallis made a decision that saved the day for the British. Over O'Hara's protests he ordered his artillery to fire grapeshot into the struggling mass of soldiery on the hill. He knew that some British troops would be killed and wounded, but he believed that this was the only way to turn back the Americans. He was relying on the discipline of British regulars to stand firm despite casualties from their own guns.

The tactic worked. The Americans fell back to regroup, and this enabled the British to do likewise. But Cornwallis gave his tired and hungry men no respite. He ordered one final assault. As the British again moved forward, Greene was afraid that his own troops might not hold their positions. He ordered a withdrawal. Firing as they pulled back, the Virginia Continentals again repulsed an attack by Webster's brigade; Webster himself fell, fatally wounded.

Guilford was a hard-fought battle. As often when two sides are evenly matched, casualties were high. British losses were about twice as great as those of the Americans, which was to be expected, since they were the attackers. Cornwallis lost at least 25 percent of his entire army. Official admitted losses were 93 British killed and 439 wounded; 78 Americans were reported killed and 183 wounded. Losses among British officers, easy to pick out by their epaulets, gold braid, and sword belts, were particularly high.

Cornwallis had driven Greene from the field and could rightly claim to have won the Battle of Guilford Courthouse. But the battle left the British in a far worse situation than the Americans. Cornwallis knew he could not afford to fight another such battle, and he was isolated in a hostile countryside. He was forced to withdraw all the way to the British-controlled port of Wilmington.

Although Greene and his men could be proud of their performance, he had been outgeneraled. His units had been unable to coordinate their action and he had missed two opportunities to destroy Cornwallis' army because of overcaution.

The rest of Greene's Carolina campaign followed the theme set at Guilford Courthouse. He fought three more battles—Hobkirk's Hill, Ninety-Six, and Eutaw Springs—and the British had slightly the better of each encounter. Yet at the close of each battle, cautious Greene was in better shape than the victorious British commanders. By the end of the year he had pushed the British back into Charleston, where he blockaded them.

CHAPTER 13

Yorktown

Situation in Virginia

In the spring of 1781 General Washington was deeply concerned about the situation in his native state of Virginia. Benedict Arnold, who had been revealed as a traitor in 1780, was now a British general and was ravaging eastern and central Virginia. Cornwallis was marching northward from Wilmington.

Responding to Arnold's depredations, Washington sent the young French volunteer Major General Lafayette to Virginia with three regiments of Continental light infantry, about 1,200 men. Then, realizing that Lafayette was badly outnumbered, he sent General "Mad Anthony" Wayne south with about 1,000 more men. Since Lafayette had been joined by about 1,800 militia in Virginia, the American force in Virginia totaled about 4,000 when Wayne joined the Frenchman on June 10, south of the Rapidan River. A few weeks earlier, however, Cornwallis and Arnold had combined forces at Petersburg, giving the British a strength of over 7,000 men in Virginia.

Aggressive Cornwallis was meanwhile engaged in a debate by letter with cautious Clinton, his superior. Cornwallis felt that with more reinforcements he could recover all of Virginia for the king. Clinton, however, held back, ordering raids and harassment only. Without more troops, Cornwallis was reluctant to stay very far from the sea in central Virginia, so he fell back slowly toward the Atlantic coast, arriving at Williamsburg on June 25. Lafayette followed as far as the town of West Point, about 20 miles away, where the Mattaponi and Pamunkey rivers flow together into the York.

Instead of receiving reinforcements, Cornwallis was now ordered by Clinton to send 3,000 of his own men to reinforce New York, where Clinton feared a combined French-American attack. Cornwallis regretfully headed down the Virginia Peninsula (between the York and the James rivers), toward Portsmouth, to embark the 3,000 men for New York. On the way he ambushed Wayne's brigade at Jamestown Ford, on July 6, but the skillful American escaped from the trap with light losses.

As Cornwallis was embarking the 3,000 men at Portsmouth, he received another message from Clinton, telling him that he could keep the men if he still felt he had to have them. Clinton also ordered Cornwallis to establish himself in a strong position on the Chesapeake Bay, mentioning Yorktown, then called York. Cornwallis kept his 3,000 men and moved into Yorktown on August 4. He also occupied Gloucester Point, across the York River.

Cornwallis was frustrated. He knew he did not have enough men to reconquer Virginia—and even if he had, Clinton would not let him. At the same time, Cornwallis knew that his 7,000 men were more than needed to carry out the minor raids that Clinton wanted. He was perfectly secure, of course, as long as the British fleet controlled the mouth of the Chesapeake Bay.

126

Lafayette promptly reported Cornwallis' situation to Washington, who was still blockading Clinton in New York. Washington was the one American commander who fully understood the importance of sea power in the Revolutionary War. It had been his understanding of sea power that had led to Burgoyne's surrender in 1777. In the summer of 1781 he was trying to decide whether to make a major effort against the British at New York City or in the Chesapeake Bay area, but after Lafayette's message he was leaning toward Virginia. Then came news that Admiral Count François Joseph Paul de Grasse, with a large French fleet, was sailing from the West Indies for Chesapeake Bay. He wrote Washington that he could remain there until October 15.

Immediately Washington grasped and acted on the strategic possibilities that de Grasse opened to him. Control of the sea in a crucial area was now possible. The capture of Cornwallis' entire force was also possible. Washington determined to send all available French and American land forces to surround Yorktown by land, while de Grasse held off the British navy and kept Cornwallis from escaping by sea.

Clinton had a much stronger force in New York than Cornwallis did at Yorktown. New York was too strong for Washington to attack, even with de Grasse's help, and one of Washington's two great concerns was that Clinton might learn of his plan and attack the smaller American army as it moved down through New Jersey. His other great worry was that either de Grasse's fleet or the smaller fleet of Admiral de Barras—sailing from Newport with needed French troops, guns, and supplies

—might be intercepted and defeated by the fleet of British Admiral Thomas Graves.

Isolating Cornwallis

To throw Clinton off his trail, Washington carefully prepared elaborate deceptions. All details of the move south were arranged so as to make the British expect an attack from New Jersey on Manhattan or Staten Island. The plan worked perfectly. The Americans, along with French troops under General Count Jean Baptiste de Vimeur de Rochambeau, moved out through New Jersey on August 25. Clinton did not realize that they had gone south until September 2, too late to catch them.

Washington continued to worry about the safety of the French fleets. When he reached Chester, Pennsylvania, on September 5, he learned that de Grasse, bringing with him 3,000 troops, had arrived safely in Chesapeake Bay. Nevertheless, Washington was still concerned about de Barras, and worried about the possibility that Graves might drive de Grasse out of Chesapeake Bay.

On the same morning that Washington got the news of de Grasse's arrival, the naval Battle of the Capes had in fact begun outside the entrance to the bay. It continued for six days, in alternate violence and silent maneuver. The French had the better of the encounter, and the British fleet retired to New York. This tactically indecisive naval battle settled the fates of Cornwallis' army and of the American Revolution. French control of the seas off the middle Atlantic coast was confirmed, and Cornwallis was isolated from all support.

Yorktown, however, was well prepared for the siege that Cornwallis now expected. Extensive fortifications had been built, while creeks and marshes provided natural protection. The only easy land approach to Yorktown was over a flat piece of land less than half a mile wide, called the Pigeon Quarter. Four redoubts had been built in the Pigeon Quarter, and it was also swept by guns in the main Yorktown fortifications.

Investment of Yorktown

Washington, Rochambeau, and Lafayette rode down from Williamsburg with their armies on September 28 to invest Yorktown. Washington assumed overall command, and the Americans held the right side of the line, while the French held the left side. Washington also sent a strong Franco-American contingent to contain the British force at Gloucester.

To their surprise, the allies discovered on September 30 that the British had abandoned their Pigeon Quarter redoubts; they promptly moved into the forts. These redoubts had been abandoned because Cornwallis had received news that Clinton was sending him a relief expedition. He decided that he should shorten his lines and conserve his strength while awaiting help.

The siege began in earnest during the night of October 6–7, as French and American engineers began to dig a trench parallel to the enemy's fortifications. The digging of such a "first parallel" was the first step of siege operations of the period. When the first parallel was completed, siege artillery was moved into it, and the bombardment began. At Yorktown, the French "Grand Battery" began the bombardment on October 9. Under

129

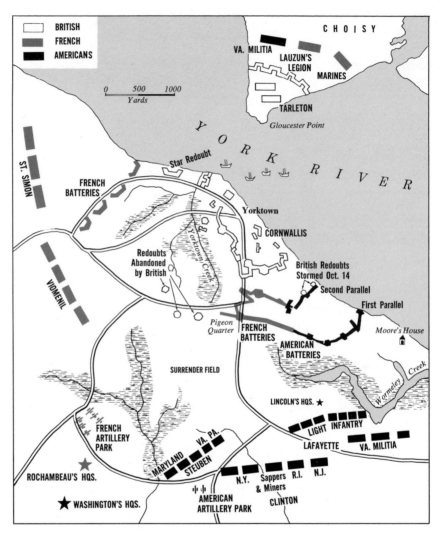

Siege of Yorktown, September–October 1781.

the cover of this fire the allied troops dug approach trenches toward Yorktown, while the British took heavy casualties from the siege guns.

The allied "second parallel" was begun the night of October 11–12. This was less than 300 yards from the British fortifications in some places, but was limited by the presence of the two powerful British redoubts, designated No. 9 and No. 10, near the river. In order to complete the second parallel, these redoubts had to be taken. Redoubt No. 10, the one closer to the river, was to be assaulted by Americans, and No. 9 by Frenchmen. These were to be surprise nighttime bayonet attacks.

Soon after dark on October 14, French Colonel de Deux-Ponts and 400 men struck No. 9 and took it after a sharp struggle made more difficult by the abatis of sharpened felled trees surrounding the redoubt. The Americans at No. 10, commanded by Lieutenant Colonel Alexander Hamilton, had an easier time, since the big siege guns had broken down much of the abatis. Both redoubts were in allied hands by 10:00 P.M. The second parallel was completed that night, and the artillery fire grew heavier and heavier as the big guns were emplaced there to begin hammering at the Yorktown defenses at short range.

In a determined effort to break out of the trap, Cornwallis ordered a sortie for October 16. A picked force of 350 men struck the second parallel before dawn at the point where the American and French sectors met. The British succeeded in spiking seven French and American guns, but were driven back by a determined French counterattack. By daylight the spikes had been removed from the touchholes, and the big guns were all in action again.

131

Surrender of Cornwallis, October 19, 1781. On foot is British Brigadier General Charles O'Hara—substituting for Cornwallis, who claimed to be ill—surrendering to American General Benjamin Lincoln, who accepted the surrender for Washington. The American commander in chief is shown to the right rear; General Count de Rochambeau, commanding the French forces, is seen to the left rear. (Perry Pictures)

This was the first and last British sortie during the siege. As the punishing bombardment continued all through the sixteenth, smashing the remains of the town and inflicting many casualties on the defenders, Cornwallis decided on an escape effort. That night he had some of his men embarked for Gloucester, where he thought he might be able to break through the relatively weak allied lines and then race northward to safety. The rest of the garrison would be ready to leave when the boats returned.

The weather, however, frustrated this last British hope. Gale winds arose, and the boats could not return across the river. The next morning the wind died, and a forlorn little convoy of troops returned across the river from Gloucester to York.

"The World Turned Upside Down"

Surrender was now inevitable. A British drummer mounted a parapet of the inner defenses and began to beat on his drum, thus signaling for a parley. A British officer, waving a white handkerchief, stepped out on the fortifications and was taken to Washington's headquarters. There he delivered Cornwallis' request for talks on surrender terms.

The American terms gave the British garrison only the limited honors of war that Clinton had granted General Lincoln at the surrender of Charleston. On October 19 the British garrison marched out, colors cased, the bands not being allowed to play any American marches, as was permitted when full honors of war were granted. According to tradition, one of the marches played was an English tune called "The World Turned Upside Down."

The British had lost 156 killed, 326 wounded, and 70 missing during the siege. They surrendered 7,247 soldiers and 840 seamen. The allies lost 53 Americans killed and 65 wounded; 60 Frenchmen were killed and 193 wounded.

The strategic impact of Yorktown was decisive. Although

133

the war dragged on another year and a half, there was little more serious fighting and there could now be no doubt of the outcome. America had won independence from Britain.

The victory would not have been possible without French assistance, particularly at sea. But Washington was the man who realized how to make the most of the help given by his French allies. It was his quick grasp of the strategic situation, his decisiveness, his excellent planning, and the smoothness of American coordination and communications that assured the victory.

Index

Abatis, 92, 93, 94, 131
Acland, Major John Dyke, 60
Acton, 12, 21
Adams, Samuel, 4, 10
Albany, 53, 54, 59, 63, 65
Alexander, Brigadier General William.
  See Stirling, Lord
Allentown, 83
Armand, Colonel Charles, 98, 100
Arms and ammunition, 7, 8, 11, 12,
  14, 20, 23, 25, 33, 41, 42, 44,
  63, 79
Armstrong, Brigadier General John,
  66, 73, 79
Arnold, Brigadier General Benedict,
  27, 54, 56, 57, 58, 59, 60, 61,
  63, 65, 125
Assunpink Creek, 41, 45, 47, 48, 49
Atlantic coast, 126, 128

Balcarres, Major Earl Alexander, 60
Barras, Admiral Count Paul Jean
  François Nicolas de, 127, 128
Barrett, James, 11
Bayonet attacks, 11, 23, 25, 33, 43,
  45, 51, 74, 93, 94, 102, 104, 112,
  113, 120, 121, 122, 131
Bedford 32, 34
Bedford Pass, 31
Bemis Heights, 55, 61
Bemis Heights, Battle of, 59–61

Bennington, 54
Bethlehem, 73
Birmingham, 43
Birmingham Meeting House, 69, 70
Bland, Colonel Theodorick, 66, 68
Blockades, 17, 27, 124, 127
Boats, 36, 38, 40, 42, 116, 133
Bordentown, 40, 41, 47
Boston, 3, 4, 6, 7, 8, 9, 10, 13, 15,
  17, 19, 20, 21, 27
Boston Massacre, 4
Boston Tea Party, 6
Brandywine, Battle of the, 65–71, 80
Brandywine Creek, 66, 67, 68, 69, 70
Breed's Hill, 19, 20, 25, 26
Breymann, Colonel Heinrich C., 55,
  61
Brinton's Ford, 66, 68
Bristol, 40, 41
British army, 4, 6, 7, 8, 10, 11, 12,
  13, 14, 15, 17, 20, 21, 22, 23,
  25, 26, 27, 28, 30, 31, 32, 34,
  35, 38, 40, 41, 48, 49, 50, 51,
  54, 55, 56, 57, 59, 60, 61, 63,
  64, 65, 68, 69, 70, 72, 73, 74,
  75, 77, 79, 80, 83, 84, 85, 86,
  87, 88, 90, 91, 92, 93, 94, 95,
  97, 99, 101, 102, 104, 107, 111,
  112, 113, 115, 116, 119, 120,
  121, 122, 123, 124, 125, 128,
  131, 132, 133
British artillery, 20, 21, 23, 25, 35, 57,

137

Grant, Major General James, 31, 32, 33, 34, 79

Grasse, Admiral Count François Joseph Paul de, 127, 128

Graves, Admiral Thomas, 128

Gravesend Bay, 30

Great Ravine, 55, 56, 61

Great Valley Road, 67, 68, 69

Greene, Major General Nathanael, 28, 30, 43, 44, 66, 68, 69, 70, 73, 74, 75, 77, 79, 87, 88, 99, 105, 106, 107, 115, 116, 117, 118, 119, 120, 121, 122, 123, 124

Groton, 21

Guilford Courthouse, 116, 117, 118, 119, 122, 123

Guilford Courthouse, Battle of, 117–124

Halifax, 28

Hamilton, Lieutenant Colonel Alexander, 51, 131

Hamilton, Brigadier General, 56, 57

Hancock, John, 10

Hand, Colonel Edward, 48

Hays, Mary. *See* Pitcher, Molly

Hazen, Colonel Moses, 66, 68

Heath, Brigadier General William, 28, 47

Heister, Major General Leopold von, 30, 31, 32, 33

Hessian artillery, 31, 32, 44, 45, 55

Hessians, 30, 31, 32, 33, 41, 43, 44, 45, 47, 54, 55, 70, 120, 121, 122

Hillsboro, 117

Hitchcock, Colonel Daniel, 51

Hobkirk's Hill, Battle of, 124

Hopewell, 83

Horses, 43, 60, 110, 112, 115

Howard, Lieutenant Colonel John E., 110, 112, 113, 115, 122, 123

Howe, Admiral Lord Richard, 28, 29, 35

Howe, Major General Sir William, 19, 20, 23, 25, 27, 28, 32, 34, 35, 40, 53, 54, 63, 64, 65, 66, 67, 68, 69, 72, 74, 75, 80, 81, 82

Hubbardtown, 54

Hudson Highlands, 59, 91

Hudson River, 28, 29, 30, 35, 53, 54, 55, 61, 82, 83, 91, 92

Hudson Valley, 53, 64

Huger, Brigadier General Isaac, 116, 118

Imports, 4, 6

Independence, 29, 38, 134

Indians, 6, 55, 56

Jamaica Pass, 31, 32

James River, 126

Jamestown Ford, 126

Johnson, Lieutenant Colonel Henry, 92, 94

Jones' Ford, 66

Kalb, Major General Baron Johann de, 98, 99, 100, 101, 102, 103, 104

King's Ferry, 92

King's Mountain, 107

Kingston, 83

Kirkwood, Captain Robert, 118, 120, 121

Knowlton, Captain Thomas, 21, 22

Knox, General Henry, 44, 77, 88

Knyphausen, General William von, 68, 70, 85, 86

Lafayette, Major General Marquis de, 82, 83, 84, 86, 88, 125, 126, 127, 129

139

Musgrave, Lieutenant Colonel
  Thomas, 77
Muskets, 11, 12, 13, 15, 16, 23, 25,
  43, 45, 70, 77, 93, 94, 115, 122
Mystic River, 20, 22

Narrows, the, 30
Neshaminy River, 65
New England, 51, 53, 91, 97
New Hampshire, 19, 20, 21, 22, 57,
  61
New Jersey, 38, 41, 42, 47, 64, 65,
  74, 82, 83, 127, 128
Newport, 127
New York City, 27, 28, 29, 34, 37,
  38, 40, 53, 63, 65, 81, 82, 83,
  90, 91, 97, 126, 127, 128
New York State, 57, 65, 98
Ninety-Six, 106, 107
Ninety-Six, Battle of, 124
North Carolina, 98, 99, 101, 102, 105,
  110, 113, 116, 117, 119, 120,
  122, 124

O'Hara, Lieutenant Colonel Charles,
  120, 122, 123
Ontario, Lake, 53

Pacolet River, 106, 109, 112
Pamunkey River, 126
Paoli Massacre, 93
Paris, 81
Patriots, 6, 7, 9, 10, 11, 15, 21, 45,
  99, 107, 111
Pee Dee River, 99
Pennsylvania, 31, 40, 41, 50, 55, 66,
  73, 93
Pepperell, 19, 21
Percy, Brigadier General Earl Hugh,
  15

Petersburg, 125
Philadelphia, 7, 27, 54, 63, 64, 65, 66,
  72, 79, 80, 81, 82, 83
Philadelphia Light Horse, 51
Pickens, Colonel Andrew, 110, 112,
  113, 115
Pigeon Quarter, 129
Pigot, Brigadier General Sir George,
  21, 23, 25
Pitcairn, Major John, 11, 14, 23
Pitcher, Molly, 88–90
Poor, Brigadier General Enoch, 57,
  60, 61
Portsmouth, 126
Prescott, Dr. Samuel, 10, 11
Prescott, Colonel William, 19, 20, 21,
  22, 25
Princeton, 44, 48, 49, 51, 64
Princeton, Battle of, 49–52, 115
Princeton College, 51
Pulaski Legion, 98, 100, 101
Punkatasset Hill, 11, 12
Putnam, Major General Israel, 19, 20,
  21, 23, 28, 30, 31, 32, 36, 112
Pyle's Ford, 66

Quebec, 27, 105

Rall, Colonel Johann, 44, 45
Ramsey's Mill, 98, 99
Rapidan River, 125
Rawdon, Colonel Lord Francis, 99,
  102
Red Lion Inn, 31, 32
Redoubts, 19, 22, 23, 25, 26, 61, 129,
  131
Reed, Colonel James, 20
Revere, Paul, 9, 10
Rhode Island, 19, 63

140

142